THE
MOMENT
OF POWER

THE
MOMENT
OF POWER
Britain's Imperial Epoch

DONALD C. GORDON

University of Maryland

PRENTICE-HALL, INC., ENGLEWOOD CLIFFS, N.J.

© 1970 by Prentice-Hall, Inc., Englewood Cliffs, New Jersey

Lines from W. B. Yeats, "Easter 1916," reprinted by permission of The Macmillan Company, and also by permission of Mr. M. B. Yeats and the Macmillan Companies of London and Canada, from *Collected Poems of W. B. Yeats.* Copyright 1924 by The Macmillan Company, renewed in 1952 by Bertha Georgie Yeats.

C-13-599928-6

P-13-599910-3

Library of Congress Catalog Card Number 76-89816

Printed in the United States of America

Current Printing (last digit):
10   9   8   7   6   5   4   3   2   1

PRENTICE-HALL INTERNATIONAL, INC., London
PRENTICE-HALL OF AUSTRALIA, PTY. LTD., Sydney
PRENTICE-HALL OF CANADA, LTD., Toronto
PRENTICE-HALL OF INDIA PRIVATE LIMITED, New Delhi
PRENTICE-HALL OF JAPAN, INC., Tokyo

Preface

At the moment of this writing, the Colonial Office of the British government is no more, and even the Commonwealth Office, its successor, has gone out of business by merger with the Foreign Office. Nothing suggests more clearly what one is irresistibly tempted to call the decline and fall of the British empire. A vast political system, the central institution of the nineteenth-century world order, has passed from the scene more rapidly than anyone could have anticipated a few decades ago. And because this empire has become a historical phenomenon rather than a present-day fact, it is now possible to see some aspects of the *Pax Britannica* in sharper focus than before.

Books in the field have been largely concerned with the constitutional arrangements of the empire, and with the development of the autonomy and later sovereignty of former dominions such as Canada, Australia, South Africa, and New Zealand. But all of these nations and now many others have taken their respective places among the sovereign nations of the world, and though they may still be included in the roster of the twenty-odd states of the Commonwealth, they are entitled to have their national histories treated as such, and to be regarded no longer as satellite communities of the British structure of power. Similarly, the newly independent African nations should be placed in the setting of their continent's history, rather than being given importance simply because of the short-lived British intrusions into tropical Africa.

Yet although today such national approaches are increasingly relevant, the fact still remains that the inclusion of these multifarious races and peoples within the vast structure of the British empire profoundly influenced their national growth and development. The empire was the major international fact of the nineteenth century. Its authority and might, and its even wider influence, led to the extension of the frontiers of western life, brought hundreds of millions within the orbit of western law, and created an international economic order that greatly contributed to the material progress of the century. This work is an attempt to examine the nature and sources of its power.

Much of the emphasis of this study is on India, since outside of the British Isles themselves India was the main reservoir of British power, and the British experience in India substantially influenced British policies in other non-European parts of the empire. If this emphasis seems to be at the cost of discussion of the major white dominions such as Canada and Australia, it is essentially because in the everyday operations of the empire, though perhaps not in the crisis years of the two world wars, India was more important in the total dimensions of British imperial power than were the communities of white settlement.

DONALD C. GORDON
University of Maryland

Contents

vii

THE
MOMENT
OF POWER

1

The

Roots

of Power

He who rules on the sea will shortly rule
on the land also.

KHAIREDDIN BARBAROSSA

In 1513 the great Portuguese admiral and empire-builder, Alfonso de
Albuquerque, wrote proudly to his sovereign from the coast of India
that "at the rumor of our coming the [native] ships all vanished and
even the birds ceased to skim over the water."[1] Since less than a generation had passed since Vasco da Gama dropped anchor off the
Malabar coast of India, the words of Albuquerque suggest how swift
and decisive had been the triumph of the Portuguese over their Arab
and Indian rivals in the Indian Ocean, and how decisive also had
been the triumph of European techniques of naval warfare over those
of their Asian foes.

The ascendancy thus gained is the more remarkable if one contrasts

1

the wealth and productivity of India and Portugal. Early European visitors tended greatly to exaggerate the wealth of India, but the large population masses, the extent of Asian cities, the pomp and display of the rulers, and their use of precious metals and gems for household and decorative purposes were all very impressive. While the poverty behind this gold and silver curtain was sometimes discerned, the general impression remained one of great wealth.

Nor was Asian society lacking in technical skills. Many of the most important technical advances in medieval European life came from Asia. And European seamen, missionaries, and merchants had a better chance to learn of Asian technology as they voyaged to and settled in the East.

Ship builders in Portugal soon learned to use coir from India and tung oil from China to calk and varnish their ships. Persons interested in sailing heard about keeled and unkeeled vessels without nails, Javan ships with four masts, Chinese junks with ingenious pumps, and sailing chariots for use on land.[2]

In general, the wealth of Asia was such that European traders seeking the privilege of carrying on their business in India had approached the rulers of that land hat in hand, humbly petitioning for, rather than demanding the right to trade with their subjects.

But there was little of this humility apparent when Europeans first approached the shores of India from the sea. They were the masters of the sea, and in the control of the sea routes lay their strength. This strength proved decisive in European relationships with the Asian world. It laid the foundations of the European hegemony over the non-European world that lasted for four hundred years, and has disappeared only in the last two decades.

The European mastery of the sea came from the development of the gunned ship. The oceanic carrack and caravel, multimasted vessels carrying an increasing number of sails, supplanted the Mediterranean galley which had been powered largely by oarsmen. The change from oar to sail made available a large additional cargo space; it also meant that the vessel could carry an increasing number of guns. Thus the ship became, in the words of one historian, "essentially a compact device that allowed a relatively small crew to master unparalleled masses of inanimate energy for movement and destruction."[3]

Europeans and non-Europeans alike used artillery from the fourteenth century on, but Europeans made such improvements in the forging and use of guns that by the close of the fifteenth century they had clearly outstripped Asians in the power of these weapons. A chronicler of the reign of the Portuguese King John II reported that the king "used to spend much money in building great vessels manned with guns." Experimenting with the use of guns at sea, John learned how to increase the armaments of small vessels, and "for a long time the caravels of Portugal were very much feared on the seas."[4]

The formidable power of their arms was displayed by two of the great Portuguese commanders in the East. Albuquerque severed the sea lanes from India to the Persian Gulf and the Red Sea by the establishment of a base on the Isle of Socotra, and by the terror which his victories at Muscat and Ormuz on the Persian Gulf spread throughout the Arab world. At Ormuz, despite the fact that the Portuguese were greatly outnumbered, they "yet held their own. Cannon against cannon, they were far better gunners and shot with devastating certainty."[5] In the first two Portuguese volleys at Ormuz, they sent two large ships, with all their men, to the bottom, and the brutality of the continuing battle stained the sea red with blood. The Portuguese pushed drowning "Moors" under the water with grappling hooks. They would "tear out their bowels in such a manner that the slaughter was great among them"; one cabin boy claimed eighty of the foe as his victims.[6] When the bodies came to the surface some days later, there was a brisk business among the Portuguese in stripping the bodies of the jeweled weapons or anything else of value that might be on them. The technical superiority of the Europeans in naval conflict was not the only aspect of European life with which the people of Asia were to become more familiar.

The threat to the Arab-Indian sea lanes posed by Albuquerque's victories created an alliance between the Arabs and the Gujarati state, north of the future site of Bombay. This combination surprised and defeated a small Portuguese fleet, but Almeida, the other great Portuguese empire builder of the period, reinforced by the opportune arrival of a squadron of vessels from Europe, smashed the combined Moslem force at the battle of Diu in 1508–9. To a great degree this consolidated the Portuguese mastery of the sea lanes approaching India. The Gujarati ruler assented to an alliance with the Portuguese, who, freed from the menace to their rear, were soon to penetrate further to the East, securing command of the Straits of Malacca in 1511.

Portuguese conquests were limited to the sea; it was there that their technology gave them command. Albuquerque wrote to his monarch that "if once Portugal should suffer a reverse at sea, your Indian possessions have not power to hold out a day longer than the kings of the land choose to suffer it."[7] Clearly dominion founded on the navy alone could not last; thus the concern for the securing and maintenance of such bases as Goa and Diu. But the costs were worth it; the "mere dross," as Albuquerque put it, was so great as to repay Portugal for much of her expenditures.[8]

The policy of Albuquerque was followed by other European states in Asia for the next two centuries. There were occasional hotheads who suggested projects of land conquest and the establishment of territorial dominion, but wiser counsels generally prevailed, and the efforts of Europeans in Asia were limited to the maintenance of their sea routes, and the defense of their factories and fortifications, both in the interests of the enlargement of trade.

The European vulnerability in land warfare that prompted Albuquerque to advocate sea power and fortresses ended, however, with the development and use of effective field artillery. This provided the answer to the problem of waging war successfully against the Asian land masses. The age of Vasco da Gama was made possible by the European superiority in ships and shipboard guns; the age of Clive, and the establishment of political power on the Asian continent, by the European development of field artillery.

By the time the new techniques of warfare had arrived in India, the coming and triumph of the Moguls had created a new political situation on the subcontinent. Some twenty-eight years after Vasco da Gama dropped anchor in Calicut, the invading Moguls from central Asia had won control of much of northern India. The battle of Panipat, in 1526, led to the establishment of the Moslem Mogul dynasty; Babur the Conqueror was the first of the emperors. His grandson, Akbar, the greatest of the Mogul emperors, by fifty years of conquest and wise government brought together most of the Ganges valley and the northern Deccan into his empire. Akbar was roughly a contemporary of Elizabeth I of England; it was to the court of his immediate successor that the first emissary of the English crown came when Englishmen sought permission to trade with, and also in, India.

Though the empire of Akbar was the most extensive that India had ever known, there were still large and populous areas to the south that remained outside his authority. The people of these regions were largely Hindu, the rulers to some degree successors to the former state of south India, Vijayanagar. There were also challenges to the authority of Akbar's descendents from the Mahrattas, a warrior people of Hindu faith welded together by outstanding military chieftains, and willing to sell their fighting services to anyone able to buy.

Despite the limitations to its power suggested by the unconquered areas of the south and the troublesome Mahrattas, the Mogul empire, especially under Akbar, was a great and imposing state and one that Europeans had good reason to approach with deference. The first emissary of the English to seek trading privileges in India was not a man of courts and diplomacy. Captain William Hawkins secured a "factory," or trading post, site at Surat, but the English East India

Company that he represented was not able to use the site effectively because of the hostility of the Portuguese. It was not until Sir Thomas Roe, an Elizabethan and Jacobean merchant-politician, and a leading figure in much of the overseas trade and colonization of the time, came to India as a representative of the English Crown that the trading permission of the English company was in any way secure.

The English had not been the first European merchants to follow in the wake of the Portuguese *fidalgos*. The Dutch, foremost among the maritime people of northern Europe, had challenged the Portuguese in eastern waters from the Red Sea to Japan with increasing success. They dispatched their first fleet to the east in 1595, and followed this with twelve others between then and 1601. In 1602 they gave greater coherence to their efforts by establishing the Dutch East India Company. The Dutch attacked the Portuguese in many of the latter's most strategic positions. When they became secure in Java, they were well situated to imperil all Portuguese activity beyond the Straits of Malacca, and the Portuguese in that area were thus limited largely to swift-sailing vessels that might escape the Dutch by their speed. The Portuguese could no longer challenge the heavy gunned Dutch East Indian ships.

After the Dutch came the English. Despite the fact that the English East India Company was established before the Dutch, and that there had been English voyages to India before the founding of the English company in 1600, English maritime activity was in no way comparable to that of the Dutch. The brilliant achievements of the English buccaneers and the success of English seamen against the Spanish, especially in the defeat of the Armada, tend to magnify the negligible role of English shipping among the fleets of Europe at the close of the sixteenth century. Though an expansion in English shipping had been under way since the middle of the century, much of it was in the small vessels carrying such cargoes as fish and coal. In larger vessels, the Portuguese were still far in advance of the English. In 1572, when the Portuguese carrack *Madre de Deus* fell prey to English vessels who carried her to Dartmouth, people flocked from all parts of the land to see her, so prodigious was she compared to English ships of the period.

But the Dutch struggle for independence against Spain gave English seamen and shipowners a larger opportunity than they had had before to secure some of the carrying trade of Europe. The outbreak of that conflict in 1568, and especially the disruption of the traffic in the great port of Antwerp, the entrepôt of northern Europe, provided the English with the opportunity to fill the gap. It furnished an immense stimulus to English shipping: "The greatest change [in overseas trade] of all during the Elizabethan period was undoubtedly in the construction of an ocean-going merchant fleet."[9] England's fleet of large size ocean-going merchant vessels, ships of more than one hundred tons burden, doubled during the 1570's, the years of the greatest destruction in Antwerp. And there was a revival of interest in the construction of larger ships following the capture of the *Madre de Deus,* so much admired by so many in Dartmouth. In the beginning of the seventeenth century, the English constructed their largest vessel to date, the thousand ton *Trade's Increase,* for the employ of the East India Company. "A ship for beauty, burthen, strength and sufficiency surpassing all merchant ships whatsoever," she was still not immune from the perils of the sea and was lost on her first voyage in 1610.[10] It was a lesson to the company not to put too much capital, cash and emotional, into one vessel, and their usual ships thereafter were about half the tonnage of the *Increase.*

England's navigational techniques and skill grew with the size of its vessels and the widening of its trade horizons. But then of course there was a cosmopolitan supranational quality about the arts of navigation that ultimately transcended national boundaries. The Portuguese tried to keep some of their hard-won skills and knowledge to themselves, but their efforts to guard their secrets were defeated by the essential fraternity of seamen. Portuguese navigators offered their skill and knowledge to other nations of Europe. Further, the conquest of Portugal by Spain, and the subsequent union of the two Iberian kingdoms, led to wider dissemination of the knowledge the Portuguese had gathered from two centuries of southern and eastern voyaging. During the war with Spain, the English seizure of a great Portuguese carrack, with its charts intact, opened up much of the Portuguese knowledge to the captors.

The English were able also to make their own contribution to the art of navigation, however; they did not live by the work of others alone. The first two rulers of the Tudor dynasty, Henry VII and Henry VIII, encouraged the development of English maritime skills, though largely through the employment of foreigners. The voyages of the Cabots, for example, during the reign of Henry VII, established later English claims to parts of the New World. Henry VIII had perhaps an even greater interest in the sea than his father; he devoted much of his kingly interest and energy to the enlargement of the Royal naval force. But the position of England in this is suggested by the comment of a scholar, "In building up his royal navy Henry gave it of the best— Italian ship wrights, French pilots and German gunfounders."[11] The limited role of the king's own subjects could scarcely be more underlined.

There were Englishmen, however, as aware of the latent possibilities of the sea frontiers of their time as some of our contemporaries are of the frontiers in space. William Bourne, in the closing decades of the century, concerned himself with the two arts, navigation and gunnery, which had proved so powerful in the establishment of European power in the Eastern seas. His *A Regiment of the Sea* (regiment meant rule) and *The Arte of Shooting Great Ordnaunce* both made original contributions to the skills they discussed; and Bourne claimed in the case of the latter work, "I am the first Englishman that put foorth any booke as touching the art of gunnery."[12] Another author followed it shortly with the first work by an Englishman on naval tactics.

Not the least of Bourne's contributions was the awakening of the minds of English seamen to the need for mathematics if they were to sail the seas with accuracy. In this, Bourne was greatly indebted to the works of the outstanding mathematician of Elizabethan times, John Dee. And there were others who followed in the lines opened by Bourne. Richard Eden, William Borough, and Robert Norman among others enlarged the knowledge of English seamen and helped make the ways of Englishmen across the trackless oceans less perilous.

Supporting and sustaining this growing command of maritime skill was the expanding economy of Elizabethan England. In agricultural productivity, in growing industries, in the development and use of new technologies, the period of English history from 1550 to 1640 has been called by one outstanding authority a true Industrial Revolution.

One aspect of the industrial growth of the period was the increasing English skill in gun making. During the second half of the sixteenth century, the English ceased to be dependent on imported guns and began to produce not only for their own needs, but also for a thriving market that had opened up abroad for their artillery pieces. Technical innovations were responsible for a good deal of this shift. The most highly prized weapons both in England and on the Continent during the first half of the century had been bronze cannons; the English iron founders developed methods of making iron guns that, though still technically inferior to the bronze, were so much cheaper that this advantage outweighed the lighter weight and greater strength of the bronze. English guns were, according to Sir Walter Raleigh, "a jewel of great value," and should not be allowed to be widely sold outside the kingdom lest they fall into the hands of potential enemies. Despite efforts to restrict the sale abroad, English guns were in such demand on the Continent that a lively trade in the weapons developed. The owner of one of the largest gun foundries in the realm reported that in 1619 the Dutch bought half of his production.

With the increasing production of ocean-going vessels and the development of guns for their protection, the English merchant community had for its use two of the essentials for conducting trading ventures in the more distant seas. The guns were not intended to force open the markets of the East to English trade, but rather to protect the vessels of the East India Company from the attacks of pirates and rival European powers, especially the Portuguese. But there were other essentials for the successful conduct of trade. Voyages to such remote areas as India and the Spice Islands demanded more capital than most English trading ventures had required heretofore. And the answer to this need was the emergence of the joint stock company.

The joint stock company was a manifestation of the growing sophistication of the English financial community. The so-called regulated company, preceding the joint stock, was essentially an association of merchants joining together for the greater security of their individual trading interests. The joint stock company, on the other hand, was an association of capital, formed for conducting trade collectively in the name of the company. In this pattern, it was able to draw capital in larger quantities from many outside the merchant community. Courtiers, land holders, gentlemen, officers of government, peers, all contributed to the capital of these embryonic corporations. There were 219 contributors to the initial capitalization of the English East India Company.[13] Many of the colonization efforts directed toward America were also carried out by joint stock companies.

The growth of English command of shipbuilding and navigation, the development of guns and gunnery, the emergence of the financial means for carrying on trade in distant seas, all helped to open the sea lanes both east and west to the colonizers and traders. But for the latter, such as those of the East India Company, there was the further problem of finding goods with which to carry on their end of the trade. The East was to be the great supplier of goods for many decades; the West the great purchaser. But where was the means of purchase? Many a worried meeting of the officials and stockholders of the company was devoted to trying to answer that problem. Basically, England had little that India and the East desired. The basic English export over the preceding centuries had been wool and woollen goods, but the price of such goods in the Indian market was too high for any effective trade to develop.

Soon after its establishment at Surat, the first factory—or trading post—of the East India Company was so burdened with English woollen cloth which it was unable to sell that the company's men began to look around for new markets. Persia seemed to be a likely place for the sale of cloth, for the climate there was colder than India's. The company's efforts to secure permission to trade were successful, and the whole enterprise seemed to open up promising new markets for English goods.[14] But such ventures were not always so successful, and over the years the company found that silver bullion was its most acceptable export to India.

The vast influx of silver into Europe from the loot of the Spanish *conquistadores* and from the mines of Spanish America made the use of silver as an export commodity simpler than it would have been decades before. Silver was debased in price in Europe because of its relative abundance, and the price for it in Asia was much higher than the price in Europe. But despite this, the export of silver from Britain brought bitter criticism down upon the East India Company. Silver, and also gold, were not just commodities, but commodities of a very special importance. Many of those interested in finance and politics of the time believed that such metals were an especially significant element in the national wealth, and their export in any substantial amount aroused fears for the economic health of the kingdom. The "drain" of silver from the land for the sake of purchasing spices, silks, and other luxuries seemed to be a sale of the national defense and security for a pleasant, but nationally enervating, mess of pottage.

There were other reasons for restlessness about the loss of silver. Silver constituted the larger part of coinage circulating throughout the realm, and its disappearance from circulation had a depressing effect on prices and the movement of goods. Even those who enjoyed the luxuries bought by the silver naturally resented the activities of any great corporation that seemed to contribute to the shortage of currency, and this kept the East India Company under a constant fire of criticism.

This barrage of criticism continued through most of the seventeenth century, and on into the next. There were two possible means of escape from the problem: the discovery of some articles of English production for which there was an active market in the East, or a change in the political relationship between India and the British merchants and company operating there. Both of these were to occur during the eighteenth century, the first through the emergence of the classic Industrial Revolution, and the second through the collapse of the Mogul Empire and the sudden eruption of British political authority in its stead.

The story of these two major events in the history of Britain and its empire is too well known to need any recapitulation. But it may be worthwhile to look at some of the factors that led to the transformation of the English East India Company from a trading corporation to the powerful agency largely responsible for the government of great areas of India.

It must be stated at the outset that this change was not the result of any great shift in policy by the directors or stockholders of the company in London. They remained as mercantile in their outlook as they had been at the inception of their trade; they wanted little if any involvement with affairs of state. For this reason, among others, they opposed the suggestion of James I in 1624 that he become a participating member of the company; larger royal influence might divert the company's interests and investments from trade to political activities. To trade as peacefully and as profitably as possible was their ambition; they would have measured up admirably to the dictum of Samuel Johnson that men are seldom more innocently employed than when making money. And they did not propose to make money by force or violence; there was little of the buccaneer or *conquistador* outlook in their leadership. The company adhered to the policy suggested to it in 1619 by Sir Thomas Roe "that if you will profit, seek it at sea and in quiet trade: for without controversy, it is an error to affect Garrisons and Land wars in India." And Roe supported his suggestion by citing the "beggaring of Portugal," which had never profited by the Indies since it defended them.[15]

But it was not always possible to follow this excellent advice. The occasional threats to the security of the company's trading posts and the need for some way of policing the population that frequently crowded into them required the formation of small garrisons. In addition, some of the trading posts established were ringed with fortifications against the dangers without. The British Crown accepted the need of the company for such security in the reissuance of the charter in 1661. This accorded the company the right to send ships of war, arms, and munitions to their trading positions in India, to erect fortifications, and to recruit volunteers in England to man them. The company could enforce martial law for the discipline of those in its military service. Later reaffirmations of the charter added to the powers of the company; in 1683 it was given the power to make war and peace with any of the non-Christian nations of Asia, Africa, and America.

By the time these larger powers were in the hands of the East India Company, many of its important leaders believed that its days of peaceful trading were coming to a close and that the company might have to adopt some of the more bellicose methods of the

Portuguese and the Dutch. The relative stability created by Akbar and maintained by his two successors was disappearing, and by the close of the seventeenth century, a political leadership had emerged in India which abandoned Akbar's wise policies. Political disorder was increasing, to the peril of European trading interests.

For the English company, the threats were most apparent in Bengal and near Bombay. In the latter area, the conflict between the Moguls and the Mahrattas threatened the security of the company. The able and energetic governor of the post, Gerald Aungier, wrote to the company in 1677, "The times now require you to manage your general commerce with your sword in your hands."[16] In Bengal, another region of major company activity, there was even more trouble. A dispatch from the company's agents there complained of the treatment accorded them by local officials:

the Moghul officers are trampling on us and extorting what they please of our estate from us, by the besieging of our Factories and stopping of our boats upon the Ganges; they will never forebare doing so until we have made them as sensible of our Power, as we have of our truth and justice.[17]

Since the company's agents were rarely above some transgression of the law, there was perhaps more ambiguity in the last phrase than its authors may have intended. It clearly stated again, however, the idea that trading would have to be carried on with sword in hand.

But the East India Company really had only a very short and somewhat blunt sword to wield against the masses of men, however imperfectly led, who were controlled by the Mogul rulers. The policy of the strong right arm may succeed sometimes, that of the weak right arm seldom if ever. The puny efforts of the company in wars against the Mogul state led to nothing but humiliation for the company. The Mogul state was still too strong "to be mocked by a handful of adventurers."[18]

Despite its setbacks in India, however, and the political difficulties hedging it about in England, the East India Company was too powerful to be overthrown. It had garnered a wealth of experience in its trade with India, a knowledge of that land that none of its rivals and would-be supplanters possessed. And it continued its labors in a field that was revealing increasing signs of political weakness and disintegration. The balance of power was slowly but perceptibly swinging in favor of the West against the East, and two factors were contributing greatly to this swing: the increasing political confusion in India, and the growing technical competence of the West.

The Mogul state of India was gradually lapsing into political incoherence. The power of the occupants of the Peacock Throne in Delhi was diminishing; that of their viziers, or servants, out in the provinces of the empire was correspondingly rising. This devolution was in large part due to the costly wars fought by the last of the outstanding Mogul rulers, the emperor Aurungzeb. Aurungzeb was a religious zealot who not only carried on wars of conquest against the Hindu rulers of south India, but battled against Moslems of opposing sects as well. Some of this may have been motivated by the hope of replacing the sultan of Turkey as the leading personage in the world of Islam, an ambition, if held, that was not to be realized. At any rate, the costliness of his wars left the resources of the central government so depleted that its power to control its servants throughout the realm declined; India entered a period of feudalization, with the major servants of the state taking upon themselves more and more of the attributes of sovereignty. The emperors weakened; their viceroys grew in strength. Those whose duty it was to collect taxes for the emperor collected as usual, but kept an increasing proportion for themselves. India gradually drifted into the anarchy perhaps best detailed by Macaulay. Describing the state of India within forty years after the death of Aurungzeb in 1707, he wrote:

A succession of nominal sovereigns, sunk in indolence and debauchery, sauntered away life in secluded palaces, chewing bang, fondling concubines, and listening to buffoons. A succession of ferocious invaders descended through the western passes to prey on the defenceless wealth of Hindostan. . . .

And there was also the problem of the Mahrattas.

It was under the reign of Aurungzebe that this wild clan of plunderers first descended from their mountains; and soon after his death, every corner of his wide empire learned to tremble at the mighty name of the Mahrattas. Many fertile viceroyalties were entirely subdued by them. . . . Nor did they, though they had become great sovereigns, therefore cease to be freebooters. They still retained the predatory habits of their forefathers. Every region which was not subject to their rule was wasted by their incursions. Whereever their kettle drums were heard, the peasant threw his bag of rice on his shoulder, hid his small savings in his girdle and fled with his wife and children to the mountains or the jungles, to the milder neighbourhood of the hyena and the tiger.[19]

But Aurungzeb, in his wars of consolidation and conquest, had set for himself and for his empire an impossible task, and the weakness and disorder that followed were retribution for his folly.

As the great Mogul state was declining in strength, the power of

Europeans to affect or control the destiny of India was rising. The various trading enclaves of the European companies spotted around the coast of India were apparently nothing but fly-specks of territory when compared with the great empire, but they represented European state systems that were rapidly gathering strength and coherence. They were the agencies of a society that was fast accumulating the tools of power and conquest in its hands.

Not all of these tools were mechanical, though all reflected the increasing role that the mechanical virtues of order and uniformity were playing in European life. The quasi-anarchism of feudalism was rapidly disappearing from European political life, to be replaced by the centralized authority of the throne. Monarchs were establishing a monopolistic hold on the tools of war, for the gunpowder and artillery of modern war were too costly for any but kings to command. The habits of disciplined thought developed over the centuries were bringing rich rewards of knowledge when applied to the study of natural phenomena. And discipline again, though of an infinitely cruder variety, was the foundation of the new standing armies which were the most obvious manifestations of the power of the new state system. The architects of the great army of Louis XIV of France, Louvois and Martinet, with their emphasis on training, drill, and uniformity of equipment were the spiritual forebears of the industrial society that emerged in the eighteenth century.

At least some of this new command of nature and new ordering of society affected the position of Europeans in India. For one thing, their lines of communication with Europe became slightly less hazardous. Not that the searoads from Europe to the Indies were without peril; far from it. Nor was there any startling innovation in shipbuilding and the navigational arts. But there was a gradual refinement in both these skills. The English East India Company was slowly accumulating knowledge and understanding of the seaways to India. The officers of the company gradually learned the optimum size for their vessels. Schools of navigation sprang up around the chief seaports of the British kingdom. And the illiterate sea captains, the sea-borne equivalents of the air pilots who "flew by the seat of their pants," were replaced by men who had not simply a knowledge of the seas and its ways from experience, but an increasing command of theoretical knowledge and navigation. The distinguished British scientist, Edmond Halley, assisted the maritime world further by the publication in 1686 of the first table of the wind movements, trade and monsoon, of the globe. With such refinements of knowledge, men could embark from London or L'Orient in France with greater confidence in the successful completion of their voyage than had been possible for the generations who had preceded them.

Accompanying this increasing reliability of communication between Britain and India was the growing potency of the weapons of war that Europeans carried to the East to equip their small forces there. Changes in weaponry made the small forces commanded by the British far more formidable than their numbers would suggest. Many of the changes occurred in the use of firearms, especially of artillery. Just as the gunned ship of the Portuguese had secured the domination of the Indian Ocean for them, so now the newly created military forces trained along European lines and equipped with European weapons became the indispensable tools for the establishment of European political power in India.

Of course, it is easy to overemphasize the role of weapons alone in the establishment of British power in India. The political disintegration on that subcontinent after the death of Aurungzeb and, even more deep-seated, the long record of failure of Indians to create really viable political institutions above the village level made the land vulnerable to conquest. But it is difficult to conceive of that conquest being either attempted or successful had the weapons of war been those of the era when "trailing a pike" was the established way of making war. Europeans in India moved into a power vacuum, but they could not have done so if they had not had the weapons of modern power to assist them. Without gunpowder and artillery, European authority would have remained what it had been for centuries, essentially a matter of ports, trading posts, and naval bases.

In 1595 the Queen's Privy Council in London had ordered the abandonment of the long bow as a weapon for English forces. The action came as a bitter wrench from past greatness, for nothing had made the English more feared in war than their proficiency with that deadly and powerful weapon. But the cherished customs, though wrapped in memories of past triumphs, had to yield to the exigencies of the present. And enamored of the long bow as they were, the English lagged behind the rest of Europe in the use of gunpowder on the battlefield.

Rulers of states and commanders of armies had used the gunpowder weapons from the fourteenth century, but it was King Gustavus Adolphus of Sweden who taught Europe the full potentialities of such weapons during his short participation in the bloody Thirty Years' War. He armed many of his infantry with a lighter firearm that permitted them to do away with the supporting crutch on which most of such weapons had heretofore been rested. But it was the mobility of his artillery that made him the master of the field and victor in some of his most notable battles. A leading student of the history of war says that he was the first commander to gauge the true value of the field gun. He gave artillery pieces a much greater mobility by cutting down their length and lightening the carriage; and he regularized and reduced the number of calibres.

How quickly the English learned the lessons taught by the Swedish king is debated by historians. Their first chance to apply these lessons came in the melancholy events of the Civil War of the 1640's, but whether field artillery played a substantial role in the victory of the Parliamentarians is uncertain. Artillery did take on a more professional caste in the small post-Restoration army, however, aided by the fact that the practice of purchasing commissions, common in other branches of the service, did not prevail there. The leading historian of the British army says that by the middle of the eighteenth century British artillerists were distinguished by "the rapidity and accuracy of their fire."[20]

Just as the introduction of the gunned ship had profoundly affected the relationships between India and the West, and made possible the development of European enclaves of power along the coast line of the great subcontinent, so now the creation of small military forces, trained and disciplined along European lines and armed with European weapons, laid the basis for European political power in India. Of course, this was not done simply because the Europeans had the guns. Such weapons as they had would never have sufficed for the conquest of a petty state, let alone a great empire, had there not also prevailed the political incoherence into which India had drifted since the days of Aurungzeb. This confusion gave opportunity for the employment of weapons; it was this condition of distraction that turned what had been the peripheral power of Europeans into the central fact of Indian government.

The European military technology, of which the field gun was but symptomatic, sufficed to overcome the massed forces of Indian rulers at such decisive engagements as Plassey and Wandewash. In the first, the great Robert Clive secured for the English East India Company mastery of the great Indian region of Bengal; the second, won to a great degree by the masterful use of artillery by the English commander, Sir Eyre Coote, extended the area of English conquest to the south.

It is notable that in these engagements the small English forces were matched more against the forces of the rival French trading company than against Indians. The artillery of the opposition in both engagements was European- rather than Indian-made. This fact gives further testimony to the role that European military technics played in India; no commander, either European or Indian, could feel equipped for battle without having European-trained and equipped forces at his command.

There is a close technical connection between the military technology of the age of Clive and that of the later industrial age. The age of gunpowder and the age of steam are linked together by the fact that both used cylinders for the production and control of energy. Lewis Mumford points out that "the gun was the starting point of a new type of power machine: it was, mechanically speaking, a one cylinder combustion engine. . . ."[21] As far as the consolidation of European power in Asia was concerned, there was close connection between the triumph of military technology, as revealed by the victories of Plassey and Wandewash, 1757 and 1760 respectively, and the development of the first really successful steam engine by James Watt in 1765. The enormous accession of power to the European economy resulting from the successful harnessing of steam tipped the technological balance even more in Europe's favor. Those Asians who struggled against the growth of European power in their societies were contending not simply with Clive and other conquerors who had much of the flavor of the earlier Spanish *conquistadores* about them. With the increasing industrialization of Britain, the Asians were contending rather with the Watts and Arkwrights, the Stephensons and Telfords of the new industrial age.

Perhaps nothing suggests this as clearly as the bloody events in India one hundred years after the first notable English victories in that land. In 1857, large sections of the native army of Bengal, troops in the employ of the English East India Company, came out in revolt against their British officers and rulers. This Sepoy Mutiny, as it was then called (though some Indians today call it their first war for national independence), saw many of the native troops, trained by the British, using the artillery, the technical tool of the age of Clive, with great effect against the British. But they were defeated in the long run by that old bugaboo of Indian life, political disunity, and also by the Industrial Revolution. For the British were able to muster forces for the suppression of the uprising through the use of the telegraph and steamship, two of the more important tools of the new age of science and industry. In effect, the mutineers, even though they were highly effective in the use of the tools of the age of Clive and Coote, were defeated by the new instruments of the age of Watt, Fulton, and Morse. It was the steamship, though not without some controversy and the continued use also of sailing ships, that hastened the transfer of forces to India to assist in the quelling of the closing phases of the revolt. But more important, it was the scanty network of telegraphs existing in the land at the onset of the mutiny that enabled British administrators and officers, where they had the will and capacity to act, to forestall the spreading of the rebellion to their own territories. Nowhere was swift and decisive action more important than in the recently conquered region of the Punjab; some of the most gifted of British administrators ruled there, and within their command were some of the largest concentrations of native troops of the Bengal army. Warned by telegraph of the outbreak of revolt near Delhi, the British officials disarmed the native regiments, recruited irregular forces, and, with the control of the Punjab thus secured, were able to move British regiments in their command to the aid of their beleaguered compatriots. The resolute action taken in the Punjab saved Britons from a much more prolonged and bitter struggle in the suppression of the uprising, if it did not perhaps save British rule in India generally. As the correspondent of the *Times* (London) in the Punjab wrote,

It is not too much to say that the telegraph saved India. . . . In a moment the news [of the revolt] was flashed to Lahore and Peshawar, to Allahabad and Culcutta, to Bombay and Madras; and all British India was on the alert.[22]

The Prime Minister of Great Britain in 1857, the year of the great Indian Mutiny, was Lord Palmerston. Palmerston was a colorful and gifted personality, whose occasional rambunctious behavior and bellicose attitudes toward other European powers won him support among the British masses. He was a friend of oppressed nationalities—on the Continent. "Under Palmerston, Britain welcomed every movement of suppressed nationalities to achieve self-government."[23] But the range of Palmerstonian interest in oppressed nationalities did not extend to India. It can, of course, be reasonably argued that the Indian uprising was not that of an oppressed nationality; that India, indeed, had no national consciousness whatever. This is a view of competent present-day historians of independent India, but nevertheless, Palmerston's sympathy for peoples oppressed had some notable limitations.

If there was a strong national assertiveness in the Palmerstonian utterances and diplomacy, if his attitude toward the remainder of the world was informed with a strong *civis Britannicus sum*, with the implication that this was the highest to which mankind could aspire, this is understandable in the light of British achievements, position, prestige, and power in the mid-nineteenth century world. For Britain was now reaping the first rich harvest of rewards from her pioneering role in the creation of the industrial society; she had become "the workshop of the world." The middle decades of the century were an age of cotton, coal, and iron; in the production of cotton goods and in the export of that and iron and coal, Britain led the world with no visible challengers to her pre-eminence anywhere on the discernible track. As the economic historian, David S. Landes, has said:

This little island, with a population half that of France, was turning out about two-thirds of the world's coal, more than half of its iron and cotton cloth. . . . Her merchandise dominated all the markets of the world; her manufacturers feared no competition; she had even—in a move that marked a break with hundreds of years of economic nationalism—removed almost all the artificial protections of her industrialists, farmers and shippers against foreign rivals. What other country could follow suit? She was, in short, the very model of industrial excellence and achievement—for some, a pace setter to be copied and surpassed; for others, a superior economic power whose achievements rested on the special bounty of an uneven Providence, hence a rival to be envied and feared. But all watched and visited and tried to learn.[24]

In 1851, in the first of the World's Fairs, Britain put her industrial achievements on display in the famous Crystal Palace exposition. Millions from all over the world came to gaze and to marvel and went away impressed by the industrial prowess of the world's leading— almost the world's only—manufacturing nation. Not the least of the exposition's triumphs was that the whole show was planned and constructed in less than a year, with all the world's exhibits open on time—with the exception of the Russian.

The optimism and expectation associated with this triumphant show of man's industrial progress is best suggested by the statement of the Prince Consort Albert, who had much to do with the successful planning of the whole enterprise. Speaking while the construction was still underway, he said that the exposition would give a living picture of the degree to which man had succeeded in the great and sacred mission he was to perform in the world:

His reason being created after the image of God, he has to use it to discover the laws by which the Almighty governs His creation, and, by making these laws his standard of action, to conquer nature to his use; himself a divine instrument.

Science discovers these laws of power, motion and transformation; industry applies them to raw matter, which the earth yields us in abundance, but which becomes valuable only by knowledge. Art teaches us the immutable laws of beauty and symmetry, and gives to our productions forms in accordance to them.[25]

The effect of this sort of prodigious industrial achievement on the British mind was naturally great. There were those who deplored some of its social results; those who saw the spirit of greed rampant everywhere; those who lamented the decline in the ancient traditions of craftsmanship; those who regretted the disruption of the established relations between tenant and landlord-squire and the decline in the social spirit of the English countryside. There were also those who watched with horror the rise of the great industrial towns as they swallowed up the millions who poured in from the country to work in the smoky factories.

The great critic of so much of the spirit of the age, John Henry Newman, spoke of

that low ambition which sets every one on the lookout to succeed and to rise in life, to amass money, to gain power, to depress his rivals, to triumph over his hitherto superiors, to affect a consequence and a gentility which he had not before.[26]

But while Newman would have been joined by others such as Robert Southey, John Ruskin, William Cobbett, and Matthew Arnold in criticism of the changes wrought by industrialism and the growth of the commercial spirit, rather more typical was the attitude of those who saw much to applaud and little to deprecate in the development of the prodigal powers of production in English life. Those who rejoiced in the growth of wealth outnumbered those who saw in that growth only a threat to the social order and to the souls of Englishmen. When Macaulay pointed out that the English had created a maritime power which would "annihilate in a quarter of an hour the navies of Tyre, Athens, Carthage, Venice and Genoa together; that they had carried the science of healing, the means of locomotion and correspondence, every mechanical art, every manufacture, everything that promotes the convenience of life, to a perfection which our ancestors would have thought magical,"[27] he was much closer to speaking the mind of his times than those critics who saw death and damnation in these same circumstances.

That somewhat Anglophile American observer of the English scene, Ralph Waldo Emerson, also paid his tribute to the British pre-eminence in the world of his day.

What are the elements of that power the English hold over other nations? If there be one test of national genius universally accepted, it is success;

and if there be one successful country in the universe for the last millennium, that country is England.[28]

The modern world is theirs. They have made and make it day by day. The commercial relations of the world are so intimately drawn to London, that every dollar on earth contributes to the strength of the English government.[29]

England has inoculated all nations with her civilization, intelligence and tastes; and to resist the tyranny and prepossession of the British element, serious man must aid himself by comparing with it the civilizations of the farthest east and west, the old Greek, the Oriental, and, much more, the ideal standard.[30]

All of these extracts are from one or another of Emerson's collected essays on *English Traits*. Obviously, the flattering unctions that the English more than occasionally laid upon their own souls found solid and respectable reinforcement when they came from the pen of this distinguished American.

The fact that Britain held sway in India and other parts of the globe by virtue of its control of the new industrial skills and its superiority in the arts of war was not sufficient justification in the minds of many Britons for the fact of imperial authority. Power, with all its appeal to the undiscerning, was not its own justification. But the justifications, the intellectual and moral foundations of empire, did come from many sources.

The American sociologist William Graham Sumner once said that if you seek war, nourish a doctrine. The same comment might also be applied to empire building, for a messianic creed has frequently provided the motivation for imperial expansion. But by way of exception to this, there was comparatively little in the form of creed or doctrine involved in Britain's creation of her nineteenth-century empire. There was so little of this, indeed, that one British historian said that the empire had been put together in a fit of absence of mind.

Indeed, what doctrine there was, stemming mainly from the writings of eminent economists, was largely hostile to the creation of empire. Men like Josiah Tucker, and more notably Adam Smith and his successors, argued that the disadvantages of empire outweighed the gains. This view received notable reinforcement when Britain gained the trade benefits of the Industrial Revolution. Britain made the goods the world wanted; why should she limit her sales to an empire, be it ever so extensive, when all the world was her oyster? British economists urged the enlargement of the empire of trade, extending throughout the globe, rather than the concentration of effort on an empire of territory. Besides, the government of territories involved one in all sorts of unwanted and contentious problems, and in the enlargement of territory there was the constant possibility of provoking war with native peoples or with other European powers. A leading spokesman of this anti-imperialist view, Richard Cobden, once said that he did not want Britain plunged into war because two drunken naval captains fell to quarrelling on the other side of the globe. The true path for England to follow was one of industrial efficiency at home and the widest possible sale of its goods abroad. Since trade was essentially a collaborative enterprise between buyer and seller, in the extension of such trade there would be a firm ground laid for peace, as opposed to the risks of war in the government and enlargement of empire. In terms of doctrine, the anti-imperialists more than held their own; there was no comparable body of doctrine favorable to the enlargement of empire during most of the century.

But doctrine, either anti- or pro-empire, was not the controlling force in imperial matters. However much the anti-imperialists might urge their countrymen to shun the temptations of power and confine themselves to seeking profit in quiet trade, as Sir Thomas Roe had advised years before, there was the unsettling fact that Britain had the power to affect for good or ill the lives of millions of people who had fallen under her control. And with each new industrial advance, this power grew. At no time in the history of the relations between European and non-European peoples was the gap between European technology and that of other peoples as great as in the mid-nineteenth century, and for Britain it was greatest of all. Britain had the power to guide and affect the affairs of foreigners; the fact that the power she held had been achieved by the hard work, thrift, ingenuity, and enterprise of Britons in itself gave substantial justification for its use over those who had not demonstrated these same sterling virtues.

To the seduction of power was added the call of duty, "stern daughter of the voice of God." Britain's sense of responsibility toward those who came under her control in India had already been manifest in the eighteenth century, with the passing of legislation designed to bring the activities of the East India Company under government scrutiny and control, and with the prolonged impeachment, and subsequent acquittal, of Warren Hastings, the Governor General of British interests in India during the 1780's. During that trial, the great Edmund Burke, leader of the impeachment, had argued that there was no geographical morality and that it was the duty of the British government to see that India was ruled in harmony with the prevailing standards of government in Britain.

The religious reawakening in English life in the eighteenth century, stemming from the life and work of John Wesley, the founder of the Methodist movement, gave new fervor and dimension to this sense of responsibility. The Wesleyan movement was not confined to those who called themselves Methodists. Many members of the established Church of England fell under the sway of Methodist ideas; those who did are generally called the Evangelicals. The ardor of the Evangelicals for the propagation of the Christian gospel, and their intense faith that only in Christianity could men find a satisfactory moral and social order, had a profound effect on imperial policies.

Not all of this effect was good. For one thing, it tended greatly to diminish the cosmopolitan and tolerant attitude that had existed in the minds of some western peoples toward the cultures of the East. An example of this cultural tolerance is the career of Sir William Jones, one of the ablest servants of the East India Company during the late eighteenth century. Despite the burdens of his work as a judge, Jones devoted most of his energies to acquiring all the knowledge and understanding he could of Indian literature and philosophy. In this task, he was a pioneer student of Sanskrit, the parent tongue of the Indo-European languages and the classical language of Indian history. He translated much Indian literature into English, and in general might be regarded as the first European to attempt a mastery of Indian culture. Obviously, no such labor and effort would have been possible without some sympathy for Indian life and accomplishments; as he said, Europeans should not be like "the savages, who thought that the sun rose and set for them alone, and could not imagine that the waves, which surrounded their island, left coral and pearls upon any other shore."[31] But even Jones, with all his interest and regard for Indian art, lore, and philosophy, felt sure that the waves had left more "coral and pearls" on the shores of European life than they had on those of India. He commented that whoever travelled through Asia and was familiar with Indian literature "must naturally remark the superiority of European talents." He likened Europe to a sovereign princess with Asia as her handmaiden, and with grave condescension said that "if the princess be transcendentally majestick, it cannot be denied that the attendant has many beauties, and some advantages peculiar to herself."[32]

If Jones, with all his essential cosmopolitanism and affection for Indian cultural achievements, had that measure of condescension, then it is perhaps not remarkable that those with less knowledge and greater faith in their own religious certainties were not simply condescending, but highly intolerant. While we said earlier that doctrine had little part in the creation of the nineteenth-century empire, increasingly this new set of doctrines gained ground and made the English intolerant and contemptuous of their Indian subjects and their ways. William Wilberforce, a leading Evangelical and the greatest of Englishmen in the battle for the abolition of the slave trade, reflected this contempt in a call for a crusade against Indian religious beliefs and social practices.

Immense regions, with a population amounting . . . to sixty millions of souls, have providentially come under our dominion. They are deeply sunk, and by their religious superstitions fast bound, in the lowest depths of moral and social wretchedness and degradation. Must we not then . . . endeavour to raise these wretched beings out of their present miserable condition, 'and above all, to communicate to them those blessed truths, which would not only improve their understandings and elevate their minds, but would, in ten thousand ways, promote their temporal well-being, and point out to them a sure path to their everlasting happiness.[33]

Sir Stamford Raffles, founder of the great port of Singapore and an ardent empire builder in Southeast Asia, sounded a note of similar zeal for the implanting of British ways among the heathen.

It is to British manners and customs that all nations now conform themselves. . . . It appears that there is something in our national character and condition which fits us for this exalted station. I think too that there is a kind of destination of this character and condition to this service. It was the privilege of Britain to receive first the purest beams of reformed religion.[34]

There is obviously a large missionary impulse behind these words and those of Wilberforce. While they thought of this missionary activity essentially as the spread of the Christian faith, it would be difficult to separate the faith from the general body of European civilization. The missionary was not simply the herald of a new religion; he was the emissary of the whole set of values, ideas, and practices that he and those who sent him believed to be vastly superior to the ideas and practices of those amongst whom he labored.

Carlyle spoke of the two grand tasks assigned to the English people by world history:

Huge—looming through the dim tumult of the always incommensurable Present Time, outlines of two tasks disclose themselves: the grand industrial task of conquering some half or more of this terraqueous planet for the use of man; then secondly, the grand Constitutional task of sharing in some pacific endurable manner, the fruit of said conquest, and showing all people how it might be done.[35]

And that master of historical narrative, James Anthony Froude, spoke of the duty of Britain to lead as Rome had done in its heyday.

We have another function such as the Romans had. The sections of men on the globe are unequally gifted. Some are strong and can govern themselves; some are weak and are the prey of foreign invaders and internal anarchy; and freedom, which all desire, is only attainable by weak nations when they are subject to the rule of others who are at once powerful and just. This was the duty which fell to the Latin race two thousand years ago. In these modern times it has fallen to ours, and in the discharge of it the highest features in the English character have displayed themselves.[36]

This may not be messianic doctrine quite of the quality of early Islam, medieval Christianity, and twentieth-century National Socialism or Communism, but for Britons of the nineteenth century it was the best they had, and all things considered, it was sufficient for its purpose. Many a young man left the gentle slopes of Devon or the more rugged Yorkshire dales to lend a hand in bringing peace and order to warring tribes in Africa, to seek the end of the slave trade, or to carry the rudiments of education or medicine to some Pacific or Asian area, in the certain faith and conviction that he was an instrument for the bringing of civilization to those who stood most direly in need.

The sense of mission, whether grounded on condescending concern to bring the gifts of British civilization to those "without the law," or on the simple brotherly concern to share with the heathen the good tidings of Christian salvation, permeated a great deal of British policy in India during the first part of the nineteenth century. Accompanying it was a secular creed of considerable authority in British life: that of Jeremy Bentham. Benthamite utilitarianism, in its simplest formulation, sought to measure existing practices of government and values of the social order by the yardstick of "the greatest good for the greatest number." This simplistic approach had within it the seeds of revolution, for few societies could have withstood judgment based on such a creed. The Utilitarians were a disturbing and reformist element in British life; they were no less so in Indian life.

Of course, the Utilitarian way of reform and salvation was a profoundly secular one compared with that of the Evangelicals. "To them, sin was a product not so much man's unawareness of God as of poverty; the moral condition of a people was dependent on their material life."[37] And by the Utilitarian creed, efforts to abolish poverty would involve the reform of many of the traditional patterns of Indian life and the creation of mechanisms of government and production comparable to those of Britain.

One of the most potent of Utilitarian voices was that of James Mill. Mill was the outstanding disciple of Bentham; he was also the author of the solid and substantial six-volume *History of British India*. In this work, there is much condemnation of both Hindu and Moslem culture. Whereas Jones and others had discerned much in Indian life to admire, Mill, who had never set foot in India, found little to praise. The unfortunate fact was that for years Mill's *History* was regarded as the great work on India, and Mill was compared as an historian with Gibbon and Hume. Once published, "it held the field unchallenged for twenty-five years."[38] No man appointed to serve in India in any high capacity was likely to embark for that duty without either having read or made plans for reading it. Many an Englishman drew his first knowledge of India from this somewhat polluted source, nor was it easy to detect the pollution, for its ideas fitted well with the prejudices created by the headlong advances of Britain in industrial development or by the promptings of missionary benevolence.

All of this meant that early in the nineteenth century there had emerged the sense of duty, of trusteeship, toward those over whom Britain had established its political authority. Future generations might look back upon this as just so much hypocrisy, disguising the psychological satisfactions of exercising authority over those regarded as inferior, and hiding the economic realities of exploitation. But these truths, if truths they are, were as yet unrecognized, and most of those who went from Britain's cosy isle to the far corners of the globe to administer the affairs of empire did so with a sense of duty and responsibility toward those whom they ruled. It is notable that on what may well have been the first occasion in which the word "imperialism" was used in British life in the sense common to us today, it was associated with unpleasant duties. It was defined as "the consciousness that it is sometimes a binding duty to perform highly irksome or offensive tasks, such as the defence of Canada or the government of Ireland."[39] And the writer might easily have added to the list such matters as the conversion of the heathen, the eradication of the slave trade, the ending of piracy, and the maintenance of peace and law among uncounted millions.

Of all the factors, however, contributing to British smugness about the "Providential wisdom" implicit in the fact of their authority in India and throughout the globe, none was more important than the fact that they *were* ruling, and that most of their subjects accepted this quietly. Nothing was more potent in giving the British a good opinion of themselves and their conduct, and a condescending opinion toward those who acquiesced in a status of political subordination that Britons themselves would have struggled against bitterly. Indeed, a discerning Indian remarked that "one should not expect a sturdy Englishman to be respectful to a race of men who could be subjected to foreign rule by a handful of swordsmen and writers coming from across the high seas."[40]

Reinforcing and rationalizing the authority that Europeans held over non-Europeans were the doctrines of racial superiority. Of course, great care is needed today in the discussion of such a topic. The racialistic nonsense of the Nazis in Germany, translated into policies of genocide and torture on an unparalleled scale, colors the thought of many who encounter racialism in any form in the nineteenth century. But the racialism of previous centuries was of another character. In the eighteenth and nineteenth centuries, race became increasingly important as an explanation of the differences between the cultural levels of people in various parts of the globe. And the acceptance of the ideas of immutable racial difference tended to deprive the whole imperial enterprise of much of its former hopeful justification. British rulers of India in the decades before such racialism took hold had looked forward to the time when British government and reforms in India would allow the Indians to govern themselves and the British to withdraw from the onerous responsibility that had fallen to them. Sir Thomas Munro, military leader and Governor of the province of Madras, had written in 1824 that Britain

. . . should look upon India, not as a temporary possession, but as one which is to be maintained permanently, until the natives shall in some future age have abandoned most of their superstitions and prejudices, and become sufficiently enlightened to frame a regular government for themselves, and to conduct and preserve it.[41]

But a later great imperial pro-consul, George Curzon, said that it was vain to pretend that India could be granted self-government. "It would mean ruin to India and treason to our trust."[42]

In the earlier justifications for British rule in India, the note of trusteeship and of the civilizing role was prominent. The emphasis on such ideas perhaps reveals clearly the sense of assurance, the lack of self-doubt and questioning, and the general sense of security with which Britain assumed the responsibilities of empire. The possession of territories such as India, with the burdens that this involved, was in no sense necessary for the commercial well-being of Britain. She could still command the markets of the world by the superiority and cheapness of her products. But with the rise of powerful industrial and commercial competitors about 1870, and the onset of a severe depression in that decade, the old note of assurance that Britain had no need for territorial empire because all the globe was her empire of trade was no longer as strong and confident. Many felt that perhaps it was just as well to have satellite and subordinate states in which British goods had either legal or sentimental advantage over those of competing states. The slogan that "trade follows the flag" expressed the new attitude in its crudest form; at the highest political level efforts to weld the empire into a form of commercial union revealed the uncertainty about British capacity to compete in world trade against Germany and the United States without some form of political advantage. Whether this new sense of insecurity led to the expansion of empire, to the annexation of new lands for the sake of the trade that might be carried on there is most doubtful. But at least among the justifications of British rule over so many parts of the globe, the thought that Britain might secure trade advantages not otherwise obtainable had a new prominence.

It was, of course, easy enough to show that all this was nonsense, that trade did not follow the flag, but rather the price list, and that those who thought that the annexation of vast new territories in Africa were going to open new outlets for any important amount of British trade were dwelling in cloud-cuckoo land. But this was the later nineteenth-century Britain in which new generations of semi-literates were having an effect on the political process—a Britain that had a few years before thrilled over the bravura quality of Disraeli's diplomacy, and in so doing, had contributed the word "jingoism" to the English language. For some at least, the glibness of the slogan about trade and the flag outweighed the studies that indicated that British goods found their best markets not in Uganda or Nigeria, but in the other industrialized nations of the world.

Thus a sort of collective national selfishness added its weight to the philanthropic justifications for British power in India and increasingly in Africa. And the behavior of other powers added powerfully to the belief that Britain should hold what she had and perhaps add to it. The scramble for empire of the late nineteenth century, and the entry of Germany particularly, into the process of annexation of the world's remoter regions, gave further justification to imperial-minded Britons. Why yield up what others obviously seemed to prize? Why should the French have the Sudan, the Germans New Guinea and Southwest Africa, when the native people in those lands would be so much better off under British rule? For it was the firm British belief, and one not wholly without justification, that of all European empires, Britain's was best.

Any listing of the moral justifications Britons gave for the authority they held over vast areas of the globe and over many millions of people cannot, of course, exhaust the reasons for empire. There were innumerable private causes that gave individuals some sort of vested interests in the maintenance of empire. The chance of employment in some form of imperial service was especially important for those upper class families who looked upon public service as their prerogative. Family ties bound those in Britain with those who had migrated or who served somewhere in the broad expanses of lands under the British flag. Those in office looked at the empire through the eyes of the strategists and saw a series of key ports and bases making possible the effective deployment and use of British naval power.

But whatever the mixture of arguments, the existence of the empire was its own best argument. There it was, massive and powerful, peaceful and generally prosperous, comprehending the fairest part of earth and much of the most civilized portion of mankind. Its frontiers were guarded by disciplined valor, and its highways over the seas by the successors of Drake and Nelson. And throughout its vast extent the gentle but powerful influence of British laws and patterns of government held the people, if not always in loyalty, at least in acquiescence.

2

The
Limitations
of Power

The rulers of Great Britain have, for more
than a century past, amused the people
with the imagination that they possessed
a great empire on the west side of the
Atlantic. This empire, however, has hitherto existed in the imagination only.

ADAM SMITH
1774

Those who write about the British empire had best define what they
mean by that term, or they are likely to leave their readers in a welter
of confusion. The distinguished Australian historian, Sir Keith Hancock, has said that the word imperialism is a term no historian can
any longer afford to use. If there is no such injunction against the use
of the term "British empire," there are enough warning signs to make
the wary slow down and look about for some guide posts.

The Oxford Dictionary defines empire as "supreme and extensive
political dominion; absolute sway, supreme control." Webster's Col-
legiate comes closer to the bone with "a group of nations or states
united under a single sovereign rule." But while this definition may
have been true of the nineteenth-century British empire in the legal

sense, any practical politician concerned with the affairs of empire would have urged many a caveat against its uncritical acceptance. Edmund Burke spoke of the empire as "an aggregate of many states under one common head," a definition that brings us nearer to reality by the omission of the idea of sovereignty. Today, when the British empire exists only in shadowy form, and the Commonwealth, with all its varying shades of meaning, has pre-empted the scene, it is necessary to recall that even in the hey-day of imperial power there were substantial premonitory indications of the Commonwealth association that would later emerge. For the essential fact about the British empire was that during much of the nineteenth century it was an aggregate of states, a collection of communities most of whom governed themselves in those matters likely to affect their people most intimately. It was a polycentric, rather than a monolithic empire, permissive rather than coercive.

But to define the empire even as an aggregate of states under one common head limits the subject too severely for accuracy. For the nineteenth-century empire in its broadest sense was not limited to those states under one head or under the British flag. There were numerous communities in the world in which Britain held a degree of ascendency, communities which were part of what has been spoken of as the "informal empire" of trade, or which were related in other forms of association, not all of them commercial. These states looked to Britain, with all the prestige of its industrial power and its successful parliamentary government, for world leadership and as an object for emulation.

The aspect of the British empire that must be particularly stressed, however, is that only in a legal sense did the British empire "belong" to Britain. This might be so obvious a fact to those who lived in the empire or who were familiar with its structure that one risks sneers even for mentioning it. Yet during the years after the American Civil War, the erudite Chairman of the Senate Foreign Relations Committee, Charles Sumner, suggested that the claims that the United States had against Britain over the activities of the *Alabama* and the other Confederate cruisers be met by the cession of Canada to the American republic. Nor was this the only time that an American politician has advanced such an idea. The same thing was advocated by some in the aftermath of World War I, as a means by which Britain might meet its war debt to the United States.

The word "belong" is altogether too unsophisticated and deceptive to be allowed in discussing the relationship that existed between Britain and her dependencies in the nineteenth century. It is most misleading in its implication of unlimited power over the imperial estate. It is true that the government of the United Kingdom, the Imperial Government, was the sole possessor of the external sovereignty of the empire. It alone could annex territory to the empire and occasionally cede territory of the empire to other powers as it did the Ionian Isles to Greece in 1864. It alone could declare war and make treaties of peace with other sovereign powers. Only the laws of the Imperial Parliament covered the behavior of British subjects on the high seas and in foreign lands. The White Ensign flown at the stern of vessels of the Royal Navy was a symbol of that sovereignty; and when the colonies or dependencies acquired and operated vessels of war, as they occasionally did, they were allowed to fly only a Blue Ensign, a flag that carried with it no implications of sovereignty. In other words, the authority of the Imperial Government over external affairs of the empire, including those that affected the advanced colonies, was "complete and unquestioned."[1]

But however true this may have been in a legal sense, it is grossly inadequate as a description of the relations between Britain and her colonies during the nineteenth and twentieth centuries. Winston Churchill once remarked when confronted with a too concise statement about a complicated problem, "True, but not exhaustive." The authority of Britain over its colonies may have been close to absolute, in point of international law, but that is no indication of the real nature of relations between Britain and the states of the empire.

One clear fact about those relations is that in them coercive power played a relatively small part. To some degree this was but a reflection of the nature of British society itself. During the nineteenth century, the repressive and policing apparatus of the British state at home was, except in Ireland, relatively weak. Britain had by that time attained many of the objectives that other states had to seek by force of arms. She had national unity, internal free trade, and, in England, a uniform legal system and a modern currency and banking system. Those who sought such goals in other lands frequently had to look to revolutionary upheavals or the power of the armed forces to attain them, as in France or Germany respectively. Britain was in no such plight. For most Britons the power of the state was personified by the increasingly benign figure of the London "bobby"; the most prestigious of Britain's armed services, the Royal Navy, could bring influence, but little in the way of naked power, into the political arena. It is impossible to imagine a British politician, even of the most reactionary stripe, making a remark even remotely like that of the German Junker who believed that the German Emperor should always be in a position to say to an army lieutenant, "Take ten men and shoot the Reichstag!"[2]

Just as the apparatus of power was weak in British domestic affairs, so was it also in imperial relations. The British empire was not held together by any iron bands of military discipline, nor was the deployment of British soldiery throughout the empire required to hold a restless populace in an unhappy obedience. The British army of the nineteenth century was a professional force of limited size. For both officers and enlisted men there was substantial probability of service in distant parts. "The thin red line" of British troops was strung across the globe, with small detachments stationed in one British colony after another. But in nearly all instances these scattered units were essentially frontier defense forces rather than forces designed for the control of the local populace. Of course, the very presence of such troops may have had an intimidating effect on those resistant to British authority, but they were never anywhere in sufficient number to create a police state or a military dictatorship. Even when reinforced by substantial recruitment of native troops, as in India, the same applied. The Indian army could be and was used for suppression of civil disturbances, but it was never of sufficient size to overawe the local population.

This general lack of coercion in imperial relations was complemented by a wide measure of permissiveness. Many of the colonies had internal sovereignty, authority to manage their own affairs. Of course, this had been true since the beginning of the empire. The establishment of the first English legislative body outside the British Isles, in Virginia in 1619, was but a fulfillment of the policy incorporated in the charter of the Virginia Company, that those who migrated to the new land carried with them as much of the law and liberties of England as the circumstances allowed. With three thousand miles of heaving ocean between them and England, the colonists in America found that the circumstances allowed them a great deal. One of the most significant facts about the colonies of the first British empire, that which was disrupted by the American Revolution, was that every major colony had its own legislative assembly. And one of the important facts about these bodies was that invariably they reached for more and more power, regarding themselves as the local equivalent of the English Parliament.

The upheaval of the American Revolution did not seriously affect the internal freedoms of those colonies which remained in the empire. There was, of course, a strong feeling in British circles that the Revolution had developed because of the long-standing laxity of control over the thirteen colonies. They had been permitted too great a measure of power, and an "excess of democracy" in their political life had led to the growth of disaffection with the British connection. The British government made efforts in what was left of the empire to redress these faults by tighter administrative control and, as in Canada, by the creation of legislative bodies with more built-in conservative influence. It also retained the long established power of disallowance over colonial legislation, but it was exercised with restraint: ". . . non-interference of parliament in the internal affairs of the colonies was in 1801 a well-established political principle."[3] The self-restraint of the Imperial Government in dealing with colonial matters was occasionally abandoned, but the trend was clear. And the general policy was to become established constitutional practice with the implementation of the principles of the famous report of Lord Durham.

Lord Durham, who was sent to Canada in 1837 as Governor-General after outbreaks of armed violence in both Quebec and Ontario, took with him as advisers a group of men who had given more thought to colonial problems than most Englishmen in political life ever cared to do. Further, while in Canada he received excellent advice from Canadian politicians. The results appeared in the formulation of his report. With the exception of four areas of government—foreign relations, constitution making, the regulation of trade with Britain, with other British colonies, and with foreign nations, and the disposition of public lands—he urged that the powers of government be turned over without reservation to locally elected legislative bodies and executive officers who functioned under their authority. In his words, "the government of the Colony should henceforth be carried on in conformity with the views of the majority in the Assembly."[4]

The Imperial authorities did not accept the principles of the famous report immediately, but a transition from the representative government that already existed in many of the colonies to the responsible government that was suggested in the Durham Report was a natural development. In 1846, on the advice of the Imperial Government, the principle was adopted in Nova Scotia, and two years later it went into practical effect in the united provinces of Canada, that is, in Ontario and Quebec. The principle of responsible government was soon applied beyond Canada, in the Australian colonies, in New Zealand, in the Cape Colony in South Africa. And the limitations on colonial powers that Durham had suggested eventually disappeared, though perhaps not as rapidly as some of the colonial authorities might have wished. To a great degree, the principal beneficiary of this enlargement of the powers of colonial governments was the United Kingdom. It freed the officials in Whitehall of many of the problems arising in colonial societies and left those solely in the hands of local officials. It was an act of emancipation, but the emancipation was as much for the Imperial Government as for the colonies.

It is notable that this devolution of power, this conferring of self-government, extended only to the colonies with white populations. Despite the Durham Report, India was ruled autocratically during the nineteenth century, with only minimal representation of those governed in the structure of authority. Gladstone, the great liberal, deplored in 1880 that Britain had not been able to give to India "the benefits and blessings of free institutions."[5] And the Viceroy whom Gladstone and his Cabinet dispatched to India in 1880 went with instructions to inaugurate a system of local self-governing institutions in India.

Race played its unhappy part in this situation. The decades of the 1840's and the 1850's, the years during which the Canadian and Australian colonies received the powers of responsible government, were also the decades in which pseudo-scientific racial doctrines attracted the greatest degree of attention and won the widest degree of acceptance in the British and European mind. In France in 1854, Comte de Gobineau began the publication of his *Essai sur l'inégalité des races humaines*, the most influential of nineteenth-century racist statements. In Britain also, "scientific voices" gave support to the common prejudices of mankind against those of different color or culture. With the growing authority of such doctrines in the public mind there was diminishing possibility that the Imperial Government would grant the powers of responsible government to colonies where they would be exercised by non-Europeans. In India, the situation was complicated further by the British reactions to and recollections of the uprising of 1857. Britons both in India and at home concluded that premature efforts to westernize India had caused that great upheaval. India and Indians, it was felt, were not ready for modernization, nor for any form of government other than autocracy. As suggested before, it was only in the 1860's and 1880's that the first timid steps were taken toward allowing Indians to have a voice in their own government, and even this was done with little hope that anything significant would emerge, for many Britons felt that only Europeans—chiefly those of Anglo-Saxon derivation—had the capacity for self-rule.

But the tradition that Britain should prepare people for self-government, that the subjects of the Crown in British colonies should rule themselves, did not die. After responsible government had been granted to Canada, Australia, New Zealand, and South Africa, the tradition was continued in the granting of self-government to the white minorities of multiracial colonies. Thus the liberalism of responsible government was combined with the prevalent racialism of the period. During the first two decades of the twentieth century, for example, British officialdom rejoiced in the creation of the Union of South Africa, another self-governing dominion in the tradition of the Dominion of Canada and the Commonwealth of Australia. Little heed was paid to the fact that the Africans themselves, the overwhelming majority of the South African population, were excluded from the political benefits of the new state. And the same was true when responsible government was conferred on Southern Rhodesia in the 1920's.

In the light of later developments, the granting of self-government to such communities apparently should have been accompanied by reservations protecting the interests of native peoples, and requiring their inclusion in the suffrage when conditions of civilized living had been attained. The struggle between a policy directed toward the protection of native peoples and one directed toward the enlargement of responsible government was an old one in British imperial affairs. But the rise of the racialist doctrines, with all their apparent "scientific" authority, combined with the costliness of maintaining a protective attitude toward native peoples and guarding them against the encroachments of aggressive whites who brought all the apparatus and values of European society with them, caused the demise of the protective attitude. Responsible government triumphed, and the cause of the natives in multiracial communities was frequently left to the discretion and mercy of the local European minority.

In the areas where the European population was too small to be granted responsible government, the picture was much simpler. Such colonies were ruled by the governors sent out by the Colonial Office in London, assisted by local whites appointed to the Governor's Executive Council and to a local legislative body. In addition to the appointed members, some of the legislators were elected by a local suffrage that was generally predominantly white. But in such colonies, there was at least a semblance of representative government, and there was also the pressure of precedents that had seen the transformation of representative government into responsible government elsewhere. Thus, and sometimes with considerable speed, the unofficial membership of the legislative body would be enlarged until it outnumbered the officially appointed, and the suffrage would be extended until it embraced colored as well as white.

Of course, for communities moving along this established path to self-government, there was always the fact that the Imperial authorities still had the final word, and occasionally this would be heard with great emphasis in a colony. Traditional leaders of a society might be removed from office and held in custody or exiled because of their resistance to some aspect of British policy, constitutions might be suspended, and rule by governor alone re-established as in the hey-day of unalloyed imperial authority.

Such instances, however, should not be allowed to obscure the general fact that the British empire of the nineteenth and twentieth centuries was first of all a collection of states or political communities in which there was little of the police-state atmosphere. Civilized political values were more honored in the observance than the breach, and there was a broadening trend toward self-government, moving from precedent to precedent and gaining strength with each move. The shadow of racialism that lay across so much of this progress was not as grievous a sin, either in the eyes of the ruled or the rulers, as it appeared to later generations. If there were occasional instances of the use of naked power in the government of empire, they were atypical. The exercise of imperial authority was limited by the traditions of British life itself, by the caution learned from such troubles as the Indian uprising, and by the tradition that British colonial administration looked for its ultimate justification to the eventual relinquishment of power to a local viable political structure.

If the exercise of naked power was rare considering the scope of the British empire and the magnitude of its problems, this was partly due to the prevalent anti-imperial feeling that existed in British political society during the middle decades of the nineteenth century. "The first half of Queen Victoria's reign—the years from the coronation to the early seventies—was the period of lack of faith in the empire, lack of belief in its value, and lack of interest in its continuance."[6] And certainly, one might add, lack of desire for its enlargement.

This indifference, if not actual hostility, of the mid-Victorians to empire and all its attractions has led some historians to an ancillary notion that the history of empire could be neatly presented in packages labelled "The Age of Mercantilism," "Free Trade and Anti-Imperialism," and "The Revival of Imperialism." The anti-imperialist decades were thus, in this view, years of modest disclaimers and self-denial separating two periods of rambunctious territory grabbing.

This perhaps over-simplified picture and the question of the extent, or even the existence, of anti-imperialism have been subjects of considerable debate among historians of recent years. Mid-Victorian anti-imperialism, so long an unquestioned phenomenon, is now under scrutiny and open to doubt. Replacing the discussions of the decades of free trade and anti-imperialism is today's talk of "the imperialism of free trade."[7]

Of course, if the enlargement of British trade was imperialistic, then no Briton of those years could be regarded as anti-imperialist. Trade was a praiseworthy activity in everyone's mind. It meant not only the enlargement of British wealth, obviously no minor consideration, but in addition it was, to many, a means for the advancement of civilization and a major contribution to world peace. It was the faith of many ardent free traders that people who traded with each other did not fight each other, for they were bound together by mutual interests that precluded war. If the extension of trade was considered imperialistic, then even the most ardent anti-imperialists could be counted in the imperialist camp.

The argument that equated trade with empire takes on substance in those cases where trade between industrialized Europe and non-European communities could not effectively develop because of the backwardness of non-European societies. It takes two to trade, and trade can flourish only between two societies that share certain common values. It can exist only under peaceful conditions, only when life and property are relatively secure, only where contractual obligations are observed, only where there is a mutual interest in the activity. If these conditions did not exist, many Britons felt, then it was necessary to create them, either by seeking out elements in the native societies that would establish them, or by establishing them through intervention and annexation, through the use of force. As Lord Palmerston said in 1860:

It may be true . . . that Trade ought not to be enforced by Cannon Balls, but on the other hand Trade cannot flourish without security, and that security may often be unattainable without the Protection of physical force.[8]

On occasion then, physical power and the outright annexation of territory could be regarded as serving the interests of British trade and, since peaceful trade was in so many ways consonant with the extension of civilization, as serving also the cause of peace, the cause of the abolition of slavery, and in general the cause of civilization against barbarism.

But too much should not be read into Palmerston's bellicose words. Just a few years before, he had also said of the countries of the eastern Mediterranean near Egypt, "Let us try to improve all these countries by the general influence of our commerce, but let us abstain from a crusade of conquest which would call down upon us the condemnation of all the other civilised nations."⁹ This was the voice of the free trader, not that of the later imperialist.

The interests of trade might occasionally lead to war, but essentially only when policies of state were guided by men like Palmerston. And what the true believers in the efficacy of free trade, men like Cobden and Bright, thought of Palmerston and his works was all too clear: they despised him. To Bright, Palmerston with his strenuous assertions of all British rights, and the rights of all Britons, against the rest of the world, was the man who had turned John Bull into "John Bully."¹⁰

With men like Palmerston, the imperialism of free trade became an occasional reality, but for most other leaders of the time, the growth of British trade would have seemed to be working substantially against the imperialist impulse.

The occasional use of force to open doors to trade, and the fact that free-trade Britain was an expanding society seeking to push its goods into all corners of the globe, should not obscure the fact that Britain did experience an anti-imperialist phase. There was more continuity in the management of imperial affairs than the earlier view admitted, but the rhetoric of imperial affairs did change substantially. The "conventional wisdom" of free-trade England was against the enlargement of empire and in favor of relieving Britain of the costs of the imperial estate. Nor was it entirely a matter of rhetoric, unless we are to assume that most of the political leaders of Britain in the mid-nineteenth century were conscious hypocrites. They may have been carried away from their anti-imperialist moorings on occasion by the swirling tide of events, as Gladstone was about Egypt in 1882, and forced into annexations enlarging the empire. Their hands may have been forced by men on the spot whom the Imperial Government could not easily repudiate, as in New Guinea in the 1880's. But such additions to empire as were made were not the subject of gratification in British political life.

The anti-imperialist tone of British policy had its roots in the laissez-faire, free-trade school of economic thought, fathered so notably by Adam Smith. Smith's most famous work, *The Wealth of Nations*, was an exposition of the doctrines of economic liberalism, a profound challenge to the existing system of government-directed trade generally called mercantilism. To contrast the doctrines of the free-trade economists with those of the mercantilists is perhaps unfair, for the two schools differed substantially on the objectives of economic activity. The exponents of mercantilism were not united in their objectives, b t they generally assumed that economic behavior should serve national political or defense needs rather than the purely economic cause of the amassing of wealth. The concern of Adam Smith was for the establishment of conditions of economic freedom in the faith that such freedom afforded the widest opportunity for the creation of wealth and the maximum availability of goods for the consumer. But in one of his most widely noted passages, he recognized the legitimacy of some of the objectives of trade regulation, especially those of Great Britain. Smith saw justification for the laws that sought the enlargement of British shipping: "As defence, however, is of much more importance than opulence, the act of navigation is, perhaps, the wisest of all the commercial regulations of England."[11] He contended, however, that the monopolies established by the British trade and navigation laws were barriers to the most effective use of capital and labor in the production of wealth:

The monopoly of the colony trade, therefore, so far as it has turned towards that trade a greater proportion of the capital of Great Britain . . . turned it from a direction in which it would have maintained a greater quantity of productive labour, into one in which it can maintain a much smaller quantity.[12]

In this and other arguments, Smith attacked the idea that colonies were of economic advantage to the imperial power. The maintenance of monopoly in any circumstances prevented the best use of capital and labor; the maintenance of an empire on the principles of commercial monopoly not only did that, to the economic detriment of the imperial power, but also involved that power in all sorts of charges for defense and government that it would otherwise not have to bear.

Under the present system of management, therefore, Great Britain derives nothing but loss from the dominion which she assumes over her colonies.[13]

And writing as he did on the eve of the American Revolution, when the problems of the colonial connection troubled the minds of Britons, Smith advocated the relinquishment of British sovereignty over the American colonies in return for a treaty of commerce allowing for free trade with the former colonists. This, he asserted, would be more advantageous to the British people as a whole, if not to some particular merchants, than the existing monopoly of colonial trade.

During the years following the appearance of the *Wealth of Nations,* despite the interruption of social change brought about by the prolonged struggle against revolutionary and Napoleonic France, Smith's ideas of economic liberalism made substantial headway among British political and industrial leaders. The growth of British industry created a class of wealth that increasingly appreciated the values for itself in the adoption of free trade; the old system of regulation seemed a limitation on the opportunities of growing British industry, whereas a worldwide system of free trade would allow the entry of British goods into all the world's markets. And the best way of creating such a world system would be for Britain to lead by example. Armed with the support given by the industrial classes, new generations of economists labored to bring the truths of the new liberalism home to the nation's leaders. And in this instruction, there was a substantial strain of anti-imperialism. The doctrines of free trade destroyed the idea of the economic utility of empire, and the free trade advocates naturally stressed the costs of empire as an additional element of their argument.

By 1820's, anti-imperialism was no longer confined to a handful of radical, speculative writers; it was becoming at least a national mood if not a conviction. . . . A general antipathy towards further imperial expansion seems to have settled in after 1815.[14]

The weight of argument and the shifting economic circumstances of British life led to the demolition of the old system of controls over trade, and in 1846, to the abolition of the citadel of protectionist strength, the tariffs on grain imports known as the Corn Laws.

The adoption of free trade as national policy seemed to many to destroy the *raison d'être* of empire. Earl Grey, Colonial Secretary in the years immediately following the adoption of free trade, wrote that

Many of the most eager advocates of the principle of Free Trade concurred in arguing that if the colonies were no longer to be regarded as valuable on account of the commercial advantages to be derived from their possession, the country had no interest in keeping these dependencies, and that it would be better to abandon them. . . .[15]

And Grey stated that he found this argument at least plausible.

Among those who held the view Grey described was Sir Herman Merivale, Permanent Undersecretary of State for the Colonies, the professional head of the Colonial Office from 1847 to 1849. He wrote that "With the colonial trade thrown open, and colonization at an end it is obvious that the leading motives which induced our ancestors to found and maintain a colonial empire no longer exist."[16] Merivale made the above statement in 1870, almost a quarter century after the repeal of the Corn Laws, a fact that testifies to the enduring hold that the anti-imperialism of free trade had on many in British public life.

Merivale went on to say in the same article that the object of British statesmen had been two-fold: "to encourage the colonies to prepare for independence for their own sake, and at the same time to relieve the people of this country from the share which they formerly bore in contributing towards their administration and defence."[17]

It would be difficult to measure the degree of influence of the two factors alluded to by Merivale in the formation of British policy. Certainly there was an overwhelming faith in Victorian Britain in the virtues of self-help and responsibility. Applied to colonial problems, this meant that one was best serving the true interests of colonial peoples by forcing them to shoulder the burdens that went with their growing maturity. They should, for their own sake, be released from the leading strings and the protective authority of the imperial state as quickly as possible. But the relief of the people of Britain from the burdens of colonial administration was certainly not a secondary factor.

It is notable that the one portion of the empire where there was little of the general reluctance to add to the burdens of empire was India. After speaking of the prevailing lack of desire during much of the nineteenth century to extend the responsibilities of empire, the editors of the *Cambridge History of the British Empire*, three historians of repute, say "In India our attitude was different. Down to the Mutiny there was no pause in the extension of British power, and no doubt in the British mind of the necessity for our supremacy in India and of the superiority of our government over that of the Indian princes."[18] This was doubtless true, but the fact that the expansion mentioned—and the costs of any wars that might be stirred up thereby—was borne largely by the Indian and not the British taxpayer, surely played its part in creating greater British receptivity to imperial expansion.

But it must be remembered that in the British mind free trade was more than a fiscal policy; it was invested with a variety of moral values. It was associated with thrift and hard work, competitive effectiveness, individual self-reliance, an ability to stand on one's own feet and confront life's problems. And these values were felt to be as valid for governments as for individuals. The highest virtues of government policy were economy in expenditure, low rates of taxation, and the widest possible scope for individual enterprise. The fact that the Victorian state actually laid the foundations of the modern welfare state did not prevent men from clinging to these shibboleths of the conventional wisdom; and this conventional wisdom governed much imperial policy. For the preoccupation with economy as the highest virtue of government was a factor that inhibited imperial adventurousness. Extension of imperial frontiers cost money. It meant added costs of administration and lengthier frontiers to defend; there were the costs of wars that might arise from conflicts with native peoples and even from clashes with other imperial powers. And there was the

argument that the greater the empire, the greater the need for armaments. This was the argument that perhaps most raised the hackles of
the free-trade economizers, for to them bulging armaments only increased the risks of war and drained the substance of the people into
unrewarding expenditures.

This concern for economy, the hostility to government assumption
of any new tasks or duties that might lead to greater expenditures, was
not the creed of any single political party. Perhaps the Whig-Liberals,
the party led by Gladstone for so much of the Victorian period, was
the more ardent in its adherence to the creed, but few among the
opposing Conservatives would have rejected these prevailing theories
of political economy. It was the "philosophy in power" regardless of
who held office. And the spirit of caution and economy that it created
in government in London was thus directly hostile to imperial expansion.

Of course the combination of laissez-faire economics, with all its
attendant moral values, plus the traditions of colonial self-government, meant there was no possibility of the British government's
seeking to plan or direct the economic development of the imperial
estate. That was something that could best be done by the people of
the dependencies themselves; they in collaboration with British investors should develop their own economies, with the government in
Britain having little or no voice or interest in the matter. Occasionally,
for strategic or humanitarian considerations, this general rule of conduct would be set aside. Thus an act of the Imperial Parliament guar-
anteed the payment of interest of a £3,000,000 loan raised by
Canadians in London to complete the construction of a railroad regarded as essential for the defense of Canada against possible American attack. And there were the substantial expenses assumed by the
British government for the abolition of slavery within the empire and
for the suppression of the slave trade.

And there was also India, so frequently the notable exception to
generalizations about British nineteenth-century imperial policies.
There the government subsidized the construction of railroad lines.
Of course there was nothing remarkable about this in the general
history of railroad financing. Governments of practically every country
in the world subsidized railroads by one means or another throughout
the later years of the century. The novelty of the Indian situation was
that this was done with the approval of the supervisory authority of
the British government, a government that was generally hostile
toward all such aids and supports.

But such exceptions should not seriously qualify the general truth that there was no control from official London of the economic growth of the empire. That was not the business of government. The business of government was to make it possible for the trader and investor to go about his lawful ways with the greatest degree of freedom, peace, and order possible.

There was nothing particularly new about this attitude. Much of the same concern for economy prevailed in the mercantilist empire of the eighteenth century. British governments, supposedly distressed over their lack of effective authority in the colonies and the fact that the imperially appointed governors, the principal agents of imperial power, were dependent on colonial legislatures for their salaries, were at the same time staunch in their refusal to pay these governors' salaries out of the imperial treasury. They also rejected on the grounds of economy suggestions for buttressing imperial authority by stationing British troops in the colonies. This parsimonious policy may in the long run have been the wise one to pursue in an empire generally indifferent or hostile to imperial restraints, but had it been followed in the earlier decades of colonial development, before the bones of colonial freedom had hardened and the muscles of colonial self-government developed, it might have meant the creation of an empire more accustomed to the habits of imperial authority.

But this is so much speculation. The facts were that in both the eighteenth and the nineteenth century British empires the Imperial Government had a generally tight-fisted attitude toward any financial claims arising from empire save for those of war, and this policy of economy diminished the power of the Imperial Government to influence colonial development. This preoccupation with economy as the supreme virtue of government limited the reach of imperial power and shackled the authority of London over the empire.

Such attitudes led to the indifference to empire current during much of the Victorian era. For the greater part of the nineteenth century there was little if any exuberant self-congratulation in Britain that the sun was having increasing difficulty in setting on the British empire. Few Britons were really interested in empire; that was the interest of a handful of dedicated men. When, for example, such a notable achievement of imperial development as the British North America Act creating the Dominion of Canada passed the Imperial Parliament, the rank and file of parliamentarians seemed to know little and care less about the matter. A leading Canadian historian describes the circumstances of the passage of the act creating the Dominion of Canada through the British House of Commons:

The few members who watched the British North America Act of 1867 in its speedy passage through parliament could scarcely conceal their excruciating boredom; and after the ordeal was over, they turned with lively zeal and manifest relief to the great national problem of the tax on dogs.[19]

Debates on colonial matters saw a drift of members from the chambers, leaving the debate to be carried forward by the "stage army" of those who cared about such remote matters. News from the colonies received little attention in the press, save during times of wars or native disturbances. The Colonial Office was regarded as one of the lesser offices of government, one that afforded little chance to an aspiring politician to make a name for himself. The popular mind did not identify British greatness with expanding territories and responsibilities overseas, but rather with the traditions of freedom, of industrial pioneering, and growing prosperity within the British Isles.

A change was to occur later in the century. Gratification in empire for the sake of empire and satisfaction in the increasing area of the globe colored with the imperial red on the maps supplanted the essential Little Englandism of the earlier decades. But for the greater part of the century, indifference reigned outside of the select group. Nor can the growth of a later emotional imperialism really be regarded as suggesting a knowledge and concern for empire that was helpful in the formation of imperial policy. The later interest was compounded of more emotion than knowledge, more heat than light, and more attitudinizing than understanding. Some politicians sought to draw on the new attitudes for political gain, but few of those who tried were able to make any constructive use of the new interest.

By the closing decades of the century much of the previous indifference toward empire had disappeared, and this new interest and concern for empire and also for its possible expansion began to appear in British political life. The roots of this new imperialism are diverse; some have already been suggested in the discussion in the first chapter. One thing is sure, and that is that no one theory will suffice to explain this somewhat belated outburst of enthusiasm for and interest in empire. Those who have made the most earnest effort to provide a monistic explanation have been of the Marxist persuasion. And the most notable early effort of this type was made by the English socialist J. A. Hobson.

Hobson's *Imperialism*, published in 1902, has been called the "starting-point of any rational explanation" of the new imperialism.[20] For him, the tap root of the new mood of expansion was to be found in the need for the mounting sums of British capital to find new areas for profitable investment. Instead of accepting the old and deceptive slogan of trade following the flag, Hobson suggested that the flag followed capital. This theory found more dogmatic statement in Nicolai Lenin's *Imperialism: The Highest Stage of Capitalism,* published in the midst of World War I.

In general, historians have felt that the Hobson-Lenin thesis has received greater acceptance than it deserves, and that the story of late nineteenth-century European expansion and conflicting imperialism is infinitely more complex than their analysis would suggest. However, the usefulness of the linkage of capitalism, imperialism, and colonialism as a stick with which to beat some western European communities and the United States has helped to keep the thesis in the forefront of communist propaganda. And it would be folly to deny that economic factors played a substantial part in the motivation of imperial expansion. These factors did not, however, operate in the schematic manner suggested by either Hobson or Lenin, but rather more in line with the older theory that saw imperialism as a search for raw materials and markets rather than investment opportunities.*

It was inevitable that the addition of vast areas to the British empire, whatever the reasons for it, aroused greater interest in the empire and its problems than had appeared before in the century. Empire became somewhat of a popular field; the Colonial Office ceased to be the second class post it had generally been assumed to be and became a highly regarded position in the first rank of Cabinet offices. Joseph Chamberlain, the brightest of the rising luminaries in the British political field in the 1890's, took that office in preference to others when offered Cabinet rank by Lord Salisbury in 1896. The Royal Colonial Society, formed in the late 1860's by a group of Australians and others from the colonies in an effort to arouse British interest in the empire, became an increasingly active group, and its roster of membership became ever more adorned with the names of the prominent in English political and social life.

Accompanying this increasing interest were a spate of projects for the closer integration of the empire in a variety of fields. Imperial federationists of many stripes and colors appeared, with favorite projects for greater unity between Britain and the leading colonies. Closer defense collaboration, political federation schemes, and the creation of a system of free trade throughout the empire with the raising of tariff barriers against the rest of the world, were all projects that aroused enthusiasm and enlisted support among some influential elements of British public life. All of them demanded that the various colonial governments, as well as Britain, yield some measure of autonomy. And none of them was successful, at least in the way their

* For a fuller discussion of the Hobson-Lenin thesis, see Chapter 4.

sponsors had hoped for. Perhaps nothing else could illustrate quite so effectively the strong roots that self-government had struck in so many of the colonies, as this reluctance of the colonies to surrender any of their autonomy.

Projects for imperial defense collaboration date essentially from the time when the imperial government withdrew the military forces that had been stationed in many of the self-governing parts of empire during most of the nineteenth century. Edward Cardwell, the Secretary of State for War in the first ministry led by Gladstone, carried out a set of reforms that undoubtedly greatly increased the fighting effectiveness of the small British army. Among these reforms was the final withdrawal of the forces from colonies such as Canada. This withdrawal process had been underway for some time; Cardwell saw it through to its conclusion. During the years in which this withdrawal was being carried out, the general tone of British thought was still considerably influenced by anti-imperialism.

The idea that the colonies might in any way contribute to the armed might of empire entered few heads, and then only to be dismissed as fantasy. Sir Charles Dilke, one of the few politicians in Britain to take a serious interest in empire, dismissed the idea in 1868. In words that stand, in the light of later developments, as a warning against the dangers of prophecy, Dilke said:

It is not likely, however, nowadays, that our colonists would, for any long stretch of time, engage to aid us in our purely European wars. Australia would scarcely feel herself deeply interested in the guarantee of Luxembourg, nor Canada in the affairs of Serbia.[21]

Dilke failed sadly to measure colonial willingness to participate in Britain's wars. Whether from deep wellsprings of imperial loyalty, from a spirit of reckless adventurism, or from a national assertiveness that sought to secure attention by defense cooperation, drawing the sword to show their own importance, as Adam Smith said, colonial governments demonstrated increasing willingness to send forces to assist in British military operations. Of course, some were more eager than others for this. Canada, fearful during much of the nineteenth century of possible American attack, was not anxious to send any of its small trained military forces out of the country. The Australian colonies displayed no such reluctance. New South Wales, for example, dispatched military units to serve with the British in operations in the Sudan in 1885. But the real manifestation of colonial willingness to serve came in the war in South Africa against the Boer republics,

1899–1902. In that war, the British received the assistance of some eighty thousand colonial volunteers. Most of these came from the English-speaking segments of the South African population, but about thirty thousand flocked to the imperial cause from Australia, New Zealand, and Canada. Since many of these volunteers came from the rural areas of these colonies, the bush and the outback, their skills were particularly useful in the open warfare of the South African veldt.

This manifestation of imperial loyalty, as it was widely construed in England, led to delusions of grandeur on the part of some Britons. Visions of an imperial *Kriegsverein* (war alliance) danced in the heads of some Whitehall statesmen, most notably in that of Joseph Chamberlain. In the light of colonial support in the Boer War, these were not totally idle speculations. And ante-dating that by more than a decade was an agreement between the British Admiralty and the governments of the Australasian colonies that the latter would make an annual contribution, though admittedly small, to the Royal Navy in return for the maintenance of a squadron of vessels in Australasian waters. But the best that Chamberlain could obtain from the colonies in the years immediately after the Boer War was a promise for the continuation of the naval agreement with Australia and New Zealand, on a slightly more generous scale, for another ten years. It was a mighty small offering on the altar of imperial unity.

In the short span of years between the South African war and the outbreak of World War I in 1914, an increasing measure of collaboration in defense arrangements developed among the major states of the British empire. The vital word here is collaboration. Canadians, Australians, and New Zealanders were only slightly less alarmed than Britons by the apparently increasing threat of German naval power and were willing to give their support to Britain in the naval race. But this support was to be given on their terms, with conditions that attested to their growing nationalism and maturity. For there was more than imperial loyalty behind the greater willingness of the colonies to aid imperial defense. Such aid, freely given, testified that colonial societies and governments were no longer dependencies, but growing communities capable of making the sacrifices to prove their new stature. The extent of these sacrifices was not great when compared with the costs of armament borne by the Britons and Europeans, but there was some substance to the cry from Canadian leaders, especially Wilfrid Laurier, that the costs of national development in the new lands should be regarded as part of the total imperial expenses for defense since such developments, especially in railroads, added to the total strength of empire.

In the war of 1914–18 itself, the reality of the imperial tie was demonstrated by the colonial contributions and losses of both men and wealth. The various states of the empire were committed to war by the imperial declaration, but they controlled the measure of their participation in the struggle. Whether they taxed their people, or raised and sent troops into combat, were matters colonial governments alone decided. But in no case were there grounds for British dissatisfaction with the efforts of the colonial governments and people. Of course, those colonies whose people came overwhelmingly from the British Isles, such as Australia and New Zealand, displayed perhaps a greater willingness for sacrifice than those whose population was of mixed origin, such as South Africa or Canada. But even in these communities the response of the French Canadians and of the Boer elements of the population was strong. Belated efforts at conscription in Canada did not succeed in bringing many more men into the ranks.

All in all, Britons had every cause for satisfaction with the colonial effort in the war. But the essential aspect of that effort was that it was voluntary. The fruits of a free imperial relationship had been more abundant than those that might have been secured through authority or coercion. The arts of persuasion were used and occasionally forms of psychological pressure applied, but in no instance was there any denial of any of the existing privileges of empire or any discriminatory policy used against those who did not cooperate.

Paralleling the efforts to create an imperial defense system were sporadic efforts to advance of the cause of imperial trade preference. Conceived by some as a step toward making a comprehensive free-trade area out of the disparate elements of the British empire, this never became an objective of the imperial government, though it did have the powerful support of Joseph Chamberlain and others. The idea that Britain and her colonies should jointly raise tariff barriers against goods from other lands had its origin in the apparently declining fortunes of Britain as a trading nation. In the hey-day of Britain's early industrial power, it was difficult to conceive that there would come a time when she might be challenged as an industrial state. In this conviction of her abiding preeminence, Britain had moved toward and finally adopted the principle of free trade, with the happy assurance that the opening of British markets to the raw material and agricultural products of the world would in turn open the markets of the world to British manufactures. And so it did. But other industrial states arose, and while British exports rarely declined in absolute value, Britain found herself increasingly pressed by German and American competition in markets in which she had for years had a comfortable monopoly. This was true even of the markets of the British empire. From 1881 to 1900, the British proportion of the total imports in India declined from 77 per cent to 65 per cent. In the case of Canada, the comparable figures for the same period also tell of a diminishing British position in the Canadian market, with the percentage of British imports slipping from 49 per cent to 24 per cent. Elsewhere the story was the same: in Australia, from 73 per cent to 61 per cent; in South Africa, from 83 per cent to 65 per cent.

The unease in British industrial and commercial circles over this decline in Britain's relative economic strength was reflected in the 1886 hearings before a Royal Commission inquiring into the causes of the depression in trade. Among the many suggestions made to the Commission was that Britain should seek closer commercial ties with the colonial empire, and of those who urged this on the Commission there were many who spoke of a tariff union as the best way to achieve these closer ties. The idea of commercial union with the colonies was particularly appealing to spokesmen for businesses that were feeling the effects of foreign competition, as well as those already well established in colonial trade.

The Report of the Royal Commission gave no encouragement to the advocates of commercial integration. But the cause of imperial preference continued to receive some measure of support. In 1887, at the first of the Colonial Conferences, the representative of the Cape Colony in South Africa urged the imposition of a supplementary tax in addition to those already imposed by some colonial governments on non-British goods, with the addendum that the proceeds of the new imposts should go into an imperial defense fund. This was an effort to tie *Kriegsverein* and *Zollverein*, or customs union, together. But the matter had already been disposed of for the moment with the comment of Lord Salisbury, the British Prime Minister, that the issue was something too shadowy and remote to be part of their immediate consideration. The British government was not prepared to abandon free trade and, equally significantly, the colonial governments were not willing to renounce their own freedom in fiscal policy, their right to tax imports, either British or foreign, as they pleased.

Even the formidable Joseph Chamberlain could not shake loose either the British or colonial governments from these general positions. In Chamberlain's advocacy of a system of reciprocal tariff preferences throughout the empire there was more than the idea of furnishing some relief to British industry from the mounting competition of other states. He was far more politically minded than that. Chamberlain saw the policy of tariff preference rather as a means of binding the communities of the empire more closely together. As the major states of empire developed their own indigenous populations, and grew increasingly remote from Britain, there was need for something to replace the waning ties of kinship. The development of close commercial links might be the means of preserving the links of empire. It might even conceivably lead to a form of political federation or centralization.

Chamberlain's admonition that Britons both at home and in the colonies had to think imperially, fell on generally deaf ears. Those at home were still too wedded to the doctrines of free trade to be shaken from that faith, and colonial governments and peoples were learning to think nationally rather than imperially. While many of them were strongly in favor of being offered a preferred position in the British market, they were too much aware of the concerns of their own developing "infant" industries to wish to see an unimpeded flow of British goods into their markets. Few of them were willing to risk either their revenues or the possibilities of manufacturing development in their own states for the sake of the larger imperial interest.

The question of some form of imperial trade preference remained to the fore for several years. Chamberlain's advocacy of the principle won him some sympathy both in colonial and British circles, but he was not able to budge the British government from its free-trade stance. Some colonial governments granted British imports a preferential tariff rate as compared with non-British products, but at the same time they were generally careful to protect their own immature industries against the danger of too great a flow of untaxed British products. The Conservative government of Arthur Balfour was troubled and agitated by the cause, but not to the degree of abandoning free trade. And in the British election of 1906, with the triumph of the Liberals who were the party *par excellence* of free trade, the doors to any form of commercial or tariff union were, as one young member of that government, Winston Churchill, was to say, "banged, bolted and barred."

Active, though frustrated, in efforts toward greater unity in both defense and trade were many earnest and learned advocates of the principle of imperial political federation. The spearhead of the agitation for closer imperial relationship was the Imperial Federation League, founded by a group of Britons and colonials, largely English-speaking Canadians, in 1884. Obviously, any institutionalized form of political association between such scattered states as those of the British empire could only take a federal form. It was the thesis of the League that the choice confronting Britons at home and in the colonies was one between federation or disintegration. This was too extreme a position for some of the members of the League; there were those who felt that the member states of the empire should work in closer concert in defense, trade, and possibly foreign affairs, but that any form of actual federation was unattainable, even if desirable.

Prominent British political figures were willing to be identified with the movement. The second chairman of the League was Lord Rosebery, an outstanding figure in the Liberal party, and leader of that party and Prime Minister after Gladstone's resignation. Another was Edward Stanhope, a member of two Conservative governments of the period. And the movement found support in some of the colonies. Branches of the League appeared in major centers in Australia, Canada, and New Zealand.

In the minds of some colonial leaders, there were substantial attractions to be found in some aspects of a closer imperial relationship. If colonial interests and concerns could be transformed into imperial interests, then various colonial positions would be formidably strengthened. Canada would feel greater security against the pressures exerted by the giant republic to the South; Australia and New Zealand would be able to call upon the strength of Britain to support their claims to a form of Australasian Monroe Doctrine in the South Pacific.

But the British government was extremely reluctant to have its power and influence pulled into every cause that colonial ebullience might espouse. Nor were colonial governments particularly interested in shouldering the burdens of defense, a request which might reasonably accompany the granting of a voice in the shaping of imperial policy. Again, no scheme of federation devised by enthusiastic supporters of the cause could overcome the vast disparity between the population of the British Isles and that of any of the colonies. None of the senior areas of the empire had appetite for schemes of representation that left them in hopeless minority status against an array of British representatives.

While the League and its supporters failed in their larger objectives, their work undoubtedly contributed to more frequent consultations between the imperial and various colonial governments on matters of imperial concern. The major expression of this new imperial consultation was the series of Colonial Conferences, later called Imperial Conferences, and still later Commonwealth Conferences. The British government, spurred on by the revival of interest in empire and specifically by the agitation of the Imperial Federation League, summoned the first of these conferences in 1887, and they have been continued under their changed names, and with ever increasing memberships, down to the present day. But this was a far cry from the type of closer imperial connection envisaged by the leaders and members of the League.

There was considerable support both in British and colonial circles for the vague idea that some form of closer cooperation between Britain and the major dominions would be advantageous to all. But despite the fact that there were outstanding advocates of specific plans that would have given flesh and form to this general idea, it was only in defense that any real efforts were made and accomplishments won; it was in defense alone that the British government sought closer collaboration as an imperial policy. The other causes, cooperation in trade or the establishment of some form of imperial government along federal lines, never had sufficient political appeal either in Britain or in the colonies involved to win support from governments or cabinets.

Fundamentally, the failure to achieve anything in these fields was due to the long-standing tradition that the end of British imperial policy was the creation of independent states, governing their own affairs, and standing sturdily on their own feet. The trend of policy was essentially permissive and devolutionary rather than restrictive and centralizing. Centralization marked too violent a departure from established attitudes and ideas to have a strong appeal, especially in Britain, where it might mean the abandonment of the cherished policy of free trade, or in the colonies, where it could easily mean the limitation of the freedoms of colonial governments.

3

The
Apparatus
of Power

And now, tell me, where *are* the Colonies?

A NEWLY-APPOINTED
19TH CENTURY COLONIAL
SECRETARY

During the first decades of the present century, the British empire embraced an area of over ten million square miles. Its territories were scattered all about the globe; literally, the "sun never set" upon it. In northern and southern hemispheres, east and west, the British flag flew from the Arctic areas of Canada, through the warm steamy lands of India and Africa, to the coldly temperate regions of the Falkland Islands in the South Pacific, and to the southerly regions of New Zealand chilled by the winds off the Antarctic to the south.

These vast regions were occupied by a population of over four hundred million people, even more diverse than the lands in which they lived. They included the advanced and sophisticated peoples of Northern Europe, North America, Australasia, and South Africa; the so-called primitive peoples still living and dying within stone age cultures; the peoples of a rich and ancient non-European culture such as that of India. In fact the empire incorporated the greatest collection of differing peoples and cultures ever brought under one political order.

How was this vast territory ruled? What system of authority, what structure of power held all of these lands and peoples in common allegiance to a remote King-Emperor or Queen-Empress whom many had never heard of and whom only a handful would ever see? Obviously there were not as many different forms of government as there were different peoples ruled, but there were enough to complicate considerably the task of describing in any detail the system of authority within the empire. But significant institutions of authority can be mentioned and agencies of government described.

Of course, large areas of the empire were governed by their own people. As indicated above, nearly all colonies had some measure of representative government, and during the nineteenth and early twentieth centuries the major colonies settled by Europeans received responsible government: Canada first, then the Australasian colonies, and finally South Africa. The granting of responsible government to these colonies was an act of double emancipation: it granted the colonies the power to order their own internal affairs, and it freed London from the worries and responsibilities of control.

But responsible government was limited to the "white" colonies, those states that later became dominions possessed of full sovereign rights comparable to those of nations that were never under British authority. There were other communities: India, the various states of Southeast Asia, the political communities carved out of the tribal societies of Africa, the islands of the Pacific, little enclaves of British power on the verges of continental areas, such as Aden in Arabia, British Honduras in Central America, British Guiana in South America, and the islands of the Caribbean. Many of these had representative assemblies, but none had responsible government. All came under the authority of the Colonial Office or India Office in London.

Both the India Office and the Colonial Office have now gone out of business; the former when India and Pakistan received independence in 1947, and the latter when the retreat of empire had gone so far that there was little left to administer. In a government reorganization at the beginning of 1967, Prime Minister Harold Wilson abolished the Colonial Office and transferred its duties, those which still existed, to other offices of government. Thus in the reign of the second Elizabeth the flag was in effect hauled down for the colonial empire that had had its inception in the years of the first Elizabeth. The abolition of the Colonial Office went almost totally unmarked by the press of the world; the shrinkage of the empire had left little for the Office to administer, and so its demise seemed too much in the natural order of affairs to attract much notice. But in its time, it and the India Office were centers of authority, influencing if not controlling the fortunes of many of the territories and peoples under the British flag.

The first fact to confront about the structure of authority of the British empire during its greatest years is the sovereign authority of Parliament. While in many ways the empire was slowly moving towards the later Commonwealth relationship of an association of equals, the fact remains that Parliament had the legal power to legislate for the entire empire. A leading authority on colonial affairs could write in 1891, "The Imperial Parliament . . . is supreme over all the colonies, whether or not possessing Responsible Government, and can make laws upon any subject . . . ."[1]

Of course the theoretical power of Parliament must not be regarded as practical power. Indeed, this was so generally acknowledged that it would be reasonable to state that Parliament's power was bound or limited by constitutional right, and that for those colonies with responsible government, the constitutional right was that they governed themselves. With each passing decade they were freer from any Parliamentary influence in their affairs. Although this power did not disappear completely until the decades between the two world wars, it was possible to trace the line of its decline and the date of its probable demise years before the actual event. But for much of the empire, Parliament was the sovereign authority not simply in theory, but also in fact.

In the history of the colonial empire, Parliament made firm claims to sovereign authority many times. The most notable instance of this was the Declaratory Act of 1766, promulgated during the years of controversy prior to the American Revolution. In this, Parliament asserted its right to legislate for the colonies in all cases. The events of the Revolution forced a partial retreat from this position, however, and in the Renunciation Act of 1778 Parliament stated that the

King and Parliament of Great Britain will not impose any Duty, Tax, or Assessment whatever, payable in any of His Majesty's Colonies, Provinces, and Plantations, in North America or the West Indies; except only such duties as may be expedient to impose for the Regulation of Commerce . . . .[2]

with the added proviso that any revenues collected in the regulation of commerce should be returned to the colonies thus taxed.

This retreat from the extreme claims of the Declaratory Act was followed by others, even while the legal power of Parliament to legislate for the empire in matters other than taxation was theoretically maintained. In relations between Imperial authority and the colonies of white settlement, the tide ran against Imperial power so strongly that by the end of the nineteenth century the idea of Parliamentary legislation having any authority over the domestic affairs of Canada or Australia was of interest only to legal antiquarians, not to practical politicians.

This was not true, however, of Parliamentary power over the colonies that had not been granted responsible government. Canada and Australia might be regarded as virtually independent states, but what was called accurately enough the "dependent empire" embraced most of the territory of the empire and certainly the greater portion of its population. It included India and many of the British territories in Africa, Southeast Asia, the West Indies, and the islands of the Pacific. For them Parliament was in many ways actually, not just theoretically, responsible. The important debates concerning forms of government of India, for example, took place in London and not in Calcutta or Delhi, something certainly not true of such states as Canada and Australia. So for such "dependent" areas, Parliament remained the effective sovereign authority.

This does not mean that Parliament was constantly interfering in the control of such areas. Parliamentary interest in colonial or Indian problems was sporadic; any continuous interest in such areas and their problems was confined to a relative handful of Members of Parliament. It is, of course, difficult if not impossible to measure the amount of interest Parliament had in colonial and Indian affairs. Certainly it was likely to increase in response to news of crisis or conflict in the empire, but aside from such instances, there were apparently few in either Commons or Lords who had a consistent interest in Imperial matters. Parliament, though jealous of its authority, was generally quite content to leave colonial matters or the affairs of India to the administrators. The constitutional responsibility of both the Colonial Office and the India Office to Parliament was more nominal than real.

Of course, such administrators could not ignore Parliament. The political head of either the India or Colonial Office could be called into account in Parliamentary questions and debates, and such occasions could be embarrassing at times for those who had not done their homework or kept tight rein on the actions of their subordinates. They had therefore a constant sense of the Parliamentary presence in their minds; Parliament existed as a cautionary influence. Politically-minded ministers—and who among them was not—preferred to do nothing and have nothing done that might arouse a clamor in Parliament. Considering the vastness of the empire and the number of touchy problems within its borders, it was perhaps most fortunate for the average office holder concerned with colonial or Indian affairs that the average parliamentarian was much more interested in domestic than Imperial matters.* This prevailing indifference, plus the increasing relaxation of Imperial control over the white colonies, certainly made life more bearable for the Colonial and Indian Offices.

If Parliamentary intervention in colonial matters became more rare as the century wore on, the activities of the major administrative office of the Imperial Government dealing with colonial matters became greater and greater. This agency was, of course, the Colonial Office, headed by a Secretary of State. The Colonial Office of the nineteenth century was a constantly changing and shifting organism, confronted as it was with the task of adjusting to shifting attitudes towards empire in Britain, and the changing character of the empire itself. Additions of territory increased its responsibilities; the granting of greater self-government diminished them. Changing conceptions of the moral obligations of Imperial power, of the duties owed by those in authority to those over whom they ruled, gravely affected the dimensions of its responsibilities. Some of the areas of empire in the East were first administered by the government of India, and then shifted to the Colonial Office. And such technological innovations as the stringing of a network of telegraph cables around the globe, making communications with London authority so much easier and speedier, added immeasurably to the labors of the Office.

The Colonial Office emerged as an important agency of government during the years of the great contest between Britain and Napoleonic France. It was coupled for years with the administration of military affairs; the head of administration was the Secretary of State for War and Colonies. As long as the conflict with France engaged the minds and hearts of Britons, the needs of war dominated the business of the joint department. But with the establishment of peace, the colonial side of the department began to receive more attention. During the

* Sir Charles Wood, one of the ablest of the Secretaries of State for India, made the revealing statement that whenever the House of Commons meddled in Indian affairs, "it is with some English view, or from some English prejudice, and very little, indeed, from knowing anything, or caring anything, about Indian interests."[3]

decade or so after the close of the Napoleonic Wars the Colonial Office began to develop the administrative procedures and to achieve the pre-eminent place in the handling of colonial matters that it held for the remainder of the century.

But in order to secure that pre-eminence it had first to insist on its place in the management of colonial matters above other agencies of government who had long had some fingers in such affairs. It would be inaccurate to say that the Colonial Office "won" this contest, but increasingly the Colonial Office became the channel of contact between the Imperial Government and the governments of most of the British colonial areas throughout the globe. Of course there was one major exception to this, and that was India. India was never within the range of the Colonial Office's responsibilities.

Though the Colonial Office was gradually able to secure acknowledgement of its priority in colonial affairs, it never held this responsibility exclusively. There was a wide variety of colonial affairs in which the Office had to secure the collaboration of other agencies of government. The most important of these was the Treasury. In harmony with the prevailing nineteenth-century concepts of self-reliance and economy in government, it was expected that colonial governments would take care of their own needs without recourse to the Imperial Treasury and the British taxpayer. But this theory frequently clashed with the realities of colonial problems. Ambitious schemes of private settlement failed, leaving British subjects exposed to starvation or anarchy unless Imperial authority came to their aid. Problems of frontier defense were beyond the financial resources of the colonies, and the support of the Imperial Government with troops and funds was needed. The Imperial policy of seeking to protect the native peoples of South Africa or New Zealand entailed expenses that could not properly be charged against the local taxpayers. In such situations it was the Treasury in London that was called upon to make the grants or to meet the bills. But the Colonial Office could not command this; it was a matter of negotiation and political maneuver, frequently requiring a good deal of time, and complicating the life of the Colonial Office and of colonial administrators.

If the attitude of the Treasury and of British governments during the nineteenth century seemed generally miserly in contrast with the twentieth-century concern for developing societies and emergent nations, it was all part of the prevailing morality and conventional economic wisdom of the time. Reliance on the Imperial Government for aid at every turn would sap the initiative and self-reliance which alone would create a viable colonial society, or so it was generally believed, just as domestic welfare programs would vitiate the economic strength and self-reliance on which Britain's industrial prowess rested. So any grant of aid to colonies was extraordinary, given grudgingly and in as small amounts as possible. All this did nothing to make the tasks of the Colonial Office or colonial officer any easier.

In addition to the Treasury, the War Office and the Admiralty were also frequently involved in colonial matters. As will be indicated later, the British armed forces of the nineteenth century, like the American army, served chiefly in the frontier areas and fought chiefly in colonial wars. The notable exception to this was the Crimean War of the 1850's. The bulk of the army served overseas, either in the colonies or in India, and a great portion of the Navy's men and ships served in waters remote from Britain, policing the distant waters of the world. While these forces served then mainly in the colonial areas, they were not under the control of the Colonial Office. Deployment or use of military force in any threatened colonial region was a matter for the Cabinet, the War Office, or the Admirality. The Colonial Office could request or urge the dispatch of military forces to colonial regions, but it could not command. Thus there had to be a good deal of negotiation with the War Office and Admiralty whenever the colonial situation seemed to require the intervention of the armed forces of the Crown.

During the early years of the century, from 1801 to 1854, relations between the military forces and colonial governors were easier than they were to be later, for they were both finally responsible to the same man. Colonial and military affairs were both under the charge of the Secretary of State for War and Colonies, a title that indicated rather clearly the prevailing ideas about the likely use of the army. The governor of a colony and the commander of the military forces there thus came under the same political control, and possibilities of friction were lessened. But with the separation of the two posts in 1854, the governor was responsible to the Colonial Office and the commander of military forces to the War Office.

A new set of instructions was issued in 1857 in an effort to clarify the powers of the governors in the colonies. Though the governors in the colonies usually carried the title of "Commander-in-Chief," they were told in the new order that this gave them no authority over the troops, and the instructions then went on

In the event of active Military operations it exclusively belongs to the Governor to state and explain to the Officer Commanding the Troops the policy of Her Majesty's Government and the Military measures by which that policy is to be obtained, but it rests with the Officer Commanding the Troops alone to direct the execution of those measures.[4]

The intention of the dispatch seems reasonably clear: the governor in any colony, a political officer, was to establish the policies, under the authority of the Crown, for the colonial government. If those policies encountered resistance that demanded military forces for its suppression, then the governor would instruct the commander of the troops on the political objectives to be sought through the use of the troops; the tactical manner in which the troops were used in this effort was left to the judgment of the military officer. The policy was a statement of the classic dictum that war was the extension of politics. But the assumption that there is some neat and effective manner of divorcing politics and war was illusory. The political and military aspects of war can seldom be so easily sundered, and so the position of the governor as "Commander-in-Chief" was ambiguous, and relations with Imperial military forces and their commanders in his colony were often contentious.

All this, of course, meant yet again that though the Colonial Office, its political chief, and its subordinate officers both in London and the colonies were charged with the responsibility of directing the affairs of all those colonies that did not have responsible government, they were limited in many ways by the need for consultation with the cooperation from other branches of government.

There was no comparable ambiguity in the relationships between the Colonial Office personnel and the Admiralty. A colonial governor, in addition to being "Commander-in-Chief," was also "Vice-Admiral," but this gave him no authority whatsoever over the ships of the Royal Navy. The most a colonial governor could do was to request the cooperation of any local naval commander; the latter was free to cooperate or not, as he saw fit or as his instructions might allow. On any matter that involved the extensive use of naval forces in colonial waters, consultation had to occur between the Colonial Office and the Admiralty in London.

But the complications of colonial management did not end with the need for consultation with the military and naval establishments. Colonial concerns, scattered all over the globe, demanded consultation with the Foreign Office. For many years, prisoners from English and Irish jails moved in a steady flow to the Australian colonies; control over the prisoners involved the Home Office. The Attorney-General and the Solicitor-General had to be consulted on legal matters. Thus a major part of the activity of any Colonial Secretary in

London was likely to be concerned with negotiations with his political peers, and the impatient scorn with which colonial governors and their associates in the colonies waited for decisions from London should have been directed as frequently as not to agencies of government other than the Colonial Office. For behind the customary official language in which the opinions or directives of the Office were couched, "I am directed by Her Majesty, etc.," were vast numbers of memoranda moving back and forth along the labyrinthine paths of British administrative correspondence. However expeditious the Colonial Office might be, it was still at the mercy of the sluggards who might be operating in other departments.

As with every other office of government, men of varying abilities held the position of Secretary of State for Colonial Affairs, the political leadership of the Office. Contemporary criticism of the policies of the Office helped establish an idea that persisted for many years that only the second-raters of British political life held the position, that truly able and ambitious men felt that it was an inferior post and that their own political careers would suffer if they were associated with it. Admittedly the office was not regarded as of the first rank in the British political hierarchy. It had no domestic "clientele" who were involved with its activities, and its concerns were generally rather remote from the interests of the general British political constituency. But a number of able men presided over the affairs of the Office as Secretary of State, from a room, it might be mentioned, adorned by a portrait of George Washington. In many respects, it was one of the most efficient government departments in nineteenth-century British administration. Among the great men who led the Colonial Office during the first half of the century were Lord John Russell and William Ewart Gladstone, both subsequently Prime Ministers. Other Colonial Secretaries with qualities that placed them in the forefront of British political life before the close of the century were Edward Cardwell, Lord Carnarvon, Lord Granville, and the Earl of Kimberley. All of these men made their mark in other departments; all of them revealed qualities of a high order in the remainder of their political careers. Certainly there were run-of-the-mill Colonial Secretaries, but there seems little reason to doubt that the Office attracted as able a group of men as most in the structure of British officialdom.

In the lower echelons of the Colonial Office, among the ranks of the permanent officials, the Colonial Office was especially fortunate for most of the century. From the 1830's through the remainder of the century, a series of highly effective administrators gave a bureaucratic leadership to the department unsurpassed by that of any other British department of government. Under the highly skilled leadership of such permanent officers as Sir James Stephen, Sir Herman Merivale, and Sir Frederic Rogers, the management of the internal affairs of the Colonial Office was quite as effective as that of other offices of the British government.

James Stephen, the first of the outstanding professional administrators in the history of the Office, worked mightily in handling the volume of business that flowed through it. But despite the lasting impression that his long years of association and his own monumental amount of dedicated labor made on the Colonial Office, the Office, like many other agencies of government in the mid-nineteenth century, apparently functioned at a most leisurely pace. The tempo did speed up a bit when ships brought in large amounts of mail from overseas areas, but between mail days the rate of activity was so languid that one official offered a bet to his colleagues that he alone could personally do all the work of the office unaided. There were no takers. The usual working day in the 1860's was from noon to five-thirty in the afternoon, but these delightful hours were not insisted on by most bureau chiefs, and clerks and other subordinates rarely had difficulty in getting additional time off. Two months' vacation each year were allowed, but seemingly little was said if additional time were taken. All in all, the whole operation had the happy atmosphere one might expect when quite possibly the most arduous labor was picking up one's paycheck. It should be mentioned that these paychecks were not large, nor was the size of the staff that enjoyed these easy conditions of work. Over the century, and even down to the time of World War I, the size of the staff hovered between thirty and forty.

But there is really no way in which one can measure the management of the affairs of the empire, for in great degree there was no intention of having such management. The general tendency over the century was to allow greater and greater discretion to the various colonial governments in the direction of their own affairs, with the function of the Colonial Office rather limited to the furnishing of advice, and with only an occasional intervening check on colonial action. Since this was the trend, it was naturally more apparent in the later decades of the century than the earlier. In the 1830's and 1840's, it was frequently necessary for the Colonial Office to hold in check some of the activities of colonial legislatures seeking to enforce policies that ran counter to those of the Imperial Government. In the West Indian colonies, for example, the plantation and slave-holding interests that dominated the local legislatures tried to throttle antislavery agitation and had to be brought up short by the Colonial Office in the interests of free speech. Many of the colonial legislative bodies were clumsy in the drafting of laws, so that the legal skills of the Colonial Office staff had to be brought to bear on legislative drafting. In several instances, colonial legislators enacted for their colonies substantial elements of the British law without modification, not considering that what might be reasonable in the British Isles was inapplicable in a tropic colony or frontier community. Banking and currency legislation was an area in which the Colonial Office had to intervene frequently in order to prevent opportunity for fraud through simple ignorance or ineptitude in law making on the part of colonial legislative bodies.

Despite the numerous instances in which the Colonial Office acted essentially as nursemaid for colonial governments, seeking to prevent them from making too egregious blunders, the general policy was to allow a wide measure of freedom to colonial legislators; a policy of laissez-faire prevailed in colonial affairs as it did in so many other areas of British life. The basic conclusion of that great administrator, James Stephen, after years of labor in and observation of colonial administration, was that he thought it probable that the day would come when the dependencies of the British Crown would insist on being dependencies no longer, and that when the time came he did not believe that there would be a single Briton who would as much as light a match, let alone fire a cannon, to prevent such a demand.[5] Such a belief would suggest that the Colonial Office was likely to find itself without colonies to administer; that those engaged in its various labors were moving along a dead-end street. Under such circumstances, there was no incentive to enter upon bold and vigorous programs in colonial affairs that would entail burdens on the British taxpayer and saddle the personnel of the Office with additional labors that might require them to come to work before noon.

But while the major dependencies of empire during the life of Stephen did attain that greater freedom he anticipated for them, the British colonial empire had a longer life than he expected. New territories, particularly in Africa, came under the British flag. And changing conceptions of the responsibilities that Britain as an imperial power had toward those whom it ruled added to the duties of the Colonial Office. New administrative tools had to be forged to discharge these new duties. The comfortable days when retired military officers made acceptable colonial governors because their pensions could supplement low salaries, and when other offices both in Britain and the colonies could be distributed on the basis of patronage, were no longer tolerable, even though a number of able men had served under such conditions. There was growing tendency to establish a corps of professional governors, men who could look forward to a career in the colonial service in one colony after another and then to a pension for their service in the later years of their life. But while such professionalization of the governors was necessary, the increasing need for scientific services in the colonies as well as more efficient administrators led to the development of a unified Colonial Service that would provide trained and efficient officers in a wide variety of services. The creation of such a unified service had long been regarded as impracticable because the health hazards in some areas of Africa barred any system of free transfer from one colony to another. But the development of tropical medicine and the subsequent diminution of the risks to health, through the work of such men as Sir Ronald Ross and the American Walter Reed, made transfers increasingly possible.

The truly unified service, however, did not come into existence until after World War I. Trained administrators, lawyers, accountants, doctors, veterinarians, educators, agronomists, surveyors, engineers, and communication experts were recruited by the Colonial Office, given further specialist training with subvention from the Office, and assigned to service in various colonial areas. The fact that they were recruited and trained in Britain did not preclude appointments to the service from local colonial populations, and, of course, local labor formed the bulk of any local colonial civil service. But the unified Colonial Service administered by the Colonial Office furnished most of the trained men in many of the colonies, and also provided them with the cadres of qualified personnel around which a competent local service might be built.

During the nineteenth and twentieth centuries, the duties of the Colonial Office managed paradoxically both to grow and to diminish at the same time. The growth came from the territorial enlargement of the empire; the diminution from the devolving of power on to the colonies.

There was little or nothing of this constant change in the administration of that major jewel of the British diadem, India; that country was autocratically governed during most of both centuries. Though India was the home of at least three quarters of the total population of the empire, it was only toward the close of the nineteenth century, and then only in the most minimal form, that Indians were given any voice in the government of their own land. India was governed by Britons, some at home and some in India, under a system whose political morality was much at odds with the general notions of self-government that prevailed in the colonies of white settlement. In contrast to the waning power of the Imperial Government in the direction of the affairs of Canada and Australia, for example, was the indubitable fact that right down to the establishment of the independence of India and Pakistan, Britain and Britons held the reins of authority in India. Edmund Burke had once pleaded that India should not be ruled under a different morality than that which was accepted in England, that there should be no "geographical morality," but that the same standards should prevail in both Britain and India. In matters of personal principle, in honesty and personal integrity, Burke's plea was answered; the men who governed India in the nineteenth century and after were as fine and as decent a body of men as any who have held power anywhere. But they were not willing to admit that India should be governed in a manner that Englishmen generally thought of as part of their own birthright.

The reasons given in justification for this were many. India was a conquered land, and what had been obtained by the sword must be held by the sword. The traditions of native government in India were not those of laws and constitutions but rather of personal power; it was a government of men and not of laws that Indians understood and appreciated most. European government with democratic features was difficult enough for Europeans; it would be impossible for Asians. Constitutional or representative government could not be applied to a conquered land nor to Asian peoples. And so despite the pride that Britons took in the fact that their nation was in the vanguard in constitutional and orderly progress, despite the growing political democracy in Britain, and despite the granting of increasing powers of self-government to many lands of the empire, India remained autocratically ruled throughout the nineteenth century and much of the twentieth.

As in the case of the rest of the colonial empire, the fundamental sovereignty rested with the British Parliament, which began to be seriously concerned with the manner of government of the British-held areas in India about 1773, and passed the first law for effective government of these areas in 1784. For about seventy-five years, from 1773 to 1858, the British attempted to rule India through the agency of the East India Company, using the company as the chosen instrument for the task. But the outbreak of the great Mutiny in the ranks of one of the company's major armies, a convulsion sufficient to threaten British rule throughout much of India, brought the policy of the "chosen instrument" to an end.

In 1858, Parliament enacted a bill entitled "An Act for the better Government of India." By this law, Parliament ended the use of the

East India Company as an agent of the Crown for the governing of India and said that India was now to be governed directly by the Crown. The law created a new office, that of Secretary of State for India, responsible to the Parliament, as the principal executive and policy-maker for India. By what appears to have been an act of singular meanness, the expenses of the new agency, the India Office, including the salary of the Secretary of State, were charged against the Indian budget and the Indian taxpayer. The reason for this was that otherwise the appropriation for the India Office would have to come in the annual estimates submitted to Parliament by the British Government, thus quite possibly becoming subject to party disputes; and party politics should be kept out of the administration of India.

It is doubtful whether Parliament had any real control over the government of India, despite the responsibility of the Secretary of State to it for this administration. Parliament lacked "the power of the purse" over India, since the governments in India controlled the revenues raised there. Parliament received an annual report on Indian finances, and this could be the occasion of a general debate on the state of India, but aside from this, its interest in India, at least as revealed by its debates, was desultory and languid.

The Secretary of State for India directed the affairs of India from London; the principal officer of government in India was the Governor-General, later given the title of Viceroy. Of the Secretaries of State and of the Governors-General dispatched to serve in India, it can be said that they were generally admirable representatives of the British governing class. They came largely from the aristocracy; they were generally high-minded and able men. But they had differing conceptions of the British role in India. For the most part, the sense of mission that had characterized British rule during the earlier years of the century, the years before the Mutiny, had gone into decline. It still lived in the minds of some Governors-General, but in a weakened and attenuated form. The hopes that had at one time existed in the minds of many Britons in India, that India might be given institutions of representative government and then brought along the road to self-government, had faded. Most of the men in power thought that this possibility was too remote to concern themselves with; they suffered from what one historian has recently called "the illusion of permanence" about British rule in India. Indeed, an outstanding Viceroy rejected the idea of singing "Onward Christian Soldiers" during a great ceremonial occasion because it contained the lines, "Crowns and Thrones may perish, Kingdoms rise and wane," an idea that he found repugnant when surrounded by the trappings of British power in India.

Unfortunately, this attitude of political rigidity was strongest when the first real stirrings of Indian nationalism were being felt. This nationalism had developed and been nurtured in the soil of English teaching, traditions, and political ideals; those who felt its urgency, the men who were its leading advocates, were also firm in their belief that Britain and India could forge a new relationship in which their two peoples would be partners in a world-wide empire. But the essential incomprehension of the British rulers, their inability to understand the aspirations of the Indian leaders who sought nothing more than Indian self-government in continued association with Britain, killed the hopes of the latter. A new generation of Indian nationalists emerged whose thought was formed less on the traditions of British self-government and more on the revolutionary examples of other societies such as France and Russia.

During the British ascendancy, the Viceroy was assisted in his administration by subordinate governors of the several provinces of British India, and by political advisors posted in many of the hundreds of "native states" that still existed. But the steel framework of Indian administrative structure was the Indian Civil Service, a deservedly famed body of men who were the principal arm of British authority in India and in whose ranks were the officers who were most likely to be known to the Indians of the villages in the countryside.

The Indian Civil Service was never large. In 1939, for instance, there were about thirteen hundred men in its ranks, and though a few Indians had been admitted to the service, the greater number of the members were still Britons. The service was among the many gifts that the East India Company left to the Crown when the latter assumed the direct responsibility of the government of India. The company had generally managed to avoid the evils of aristocratic patronage and influence in the selection and training of its officers in India; it early laid emphasis on the need to find its personnel from the middle class rather than among the aristocracy. In 1806 the company established a training school for young men going to India in its service; there was also a language school in India for their further instruction. When the Crown took over from the company it inherited a going and, in many respects, a superior corps of trained servants.

By the time the Crown assumed power in India, entry into the Civil Service was secured only through open competitive examination, and this system prevailed through the life of the Service. On the surface, this seemed a fairer method than the patronage system that had prevailed under the company. But it was subject to manipulation of various kinds by those in power. For example, Sir Charles Wood, the second Secretary of State for India under the Crown, weighted the entrance examinations heavily toward Latin and Greek so that Oxford and Cambridge men might be favored at the expense of graduates of the Irish universities and middle class cram schools. Sir Charles infinitely preferred the gentlemen of the traditional English universities to those who might qualify from more "dubious" elements of society.

But Indians, of course, were the chief victims of this system. Despite the promises given at the time of the Crown's takeover of authority that there would be no discrimination against Indian subjects of the Crown, and that the Service would be open to all through the competitive examination system, the whole procedure was arranged to make it extremely difficult for Indians to enter. Not only did the examinations require a high level of skill in English, but they were adjusted to test the knowledge of the graduates of English public schools, and they were given only in England! One Indian managed to enter the service in 1864 and three in 1869, but even those who surmounted the numerous obstacles attached to entry found themselves regarded as outsiders and were subject to a good deal of ugly discrimination.

Later, the civil services of the various Indian provinces were open to and largely filled by Indian candidates for appointment, but despite the fact that the tone and quality of these provincial services were influenced greatly by the standards of the Indian Civil Service, they did not have its prestige.

The young Englishman who was accepted into the service did not go to India as a specialist; he was usually the recipient of the general pattern of classical education of the public school, plus two years at Oxford or Cambridge. And once in India, he was likely to be serving as the representative of the British *raj* (a Hindu term meaning rule or sovereignty) in a country area in which he was the chief tiger hunter, school inspector, roads supervisor, collector of taxes, and court of first resort in local disputes—in effect, despite his youth, the essential patriarch of the society. For those with whom he had business, and they could number in the hundreds of thousands, especially in southern India, he was the government. It says much for the character of the men and the discrimination of the selection process that few broke under the strain of the isolation, the unusual labors, the heat and dangers to health, and the personal responsibilities associated with this sort of "on-the-job" training.

In essence, the task of the young officer was to keep order, not by the use of the policeman's truncheon nor by any posse of soldiery he might command, but rather by acting as judge, father confessor, wise friend, and counsellor to the communities in his district.

Thus, in much of the empire, but particularly in India and tropical Africa, the most widely known representative of Imperial authority was a young Englishman. He was known by various titles, but on his shoulders fell the front line duties of transmitting the ways of European power to the polyglot peoples of the empire.

In some of the more settled parts of the empire, the post of District Officer carried with it some considerable perquisites and amenities. But for most the work was hard and the conditions hazardous. In parts of Africa, a manual of instruction warned the young man, very frequently only recently out of an English public school, that he should be armed against a host of unpleasant possibilities.

He is warned to provide himself with mosquito nets, waterproof sheets, pump filters, water bottles capable of holding enough for a day's drinking, hurricane lanterns and other articles of camp equipment. He must have thick stockings and strong boots for trekking and is warned not to get his feet or ankles into contact with mud or stagnant water, as these things are haunts of ankylostomiasis and bilharzia. He is advised to arm himself with a stock of medicines. He is given elementary hints as to malaria, yellow fever, dysentery, black water fever and sleeping sickness. . . .[6]

And he was given further instructions on how to deal with insects and flies that get beneath the skin and deposit their eggs to hatch there. On reading this, few could have received the impression that they were going out in the Colonial Service to enjoy the delights associated with Imperial authority and prestige; there were a great many more perils to such posts in many parts of the world than simply the risks of going out in the noonday sun, as mad dogs and Englishmen were reputed to do.

No description of the apparatus of British administration would be complete without a discussion of the device of "indirect rule" that was utilized in many parts of the empire. In 1927, the British High Commissioner in the Malaya area stated that "No mandate has ever been extended to us by Rajas, Chiefs, or people to vary the system of government which has existed in these territories since time immemorial."[7] The same might have been said by representatives of British power in many parts of India and Africa as well. The British very frequently found it to their advantage to keep intact the system of internal authority of the people they ruled, as far as that was compatible with the general peace, order, and good government of the region. Thus British authority was associated with and perhaps, to the undiscerning, partially concealed behind the traditional forms of native government

—behind the princes and rulers of the native states of India, behind the Rajas and sultans of Malayan states, and behind the emirs of northern Nigeria, for example. If the British presence and authority, represented by an Agent or Resident, diminished the authority of the local ruler, it also enhanced his power by equipping him with at least the rudimentary apparatus of the modern state.

Indirect rule can be regarded as a mixed blessing. For the British it had the reality of power without the costs of direct administration; it was thus a form of empire "on the cheap." For the native peoples it meant the maintenance of their local rulers and of the indigenous aristocracy, with the consequent diminution of revolutionary impact or cultural disturbance caused by the imposition of British authority and Western ways. But of course this meant a delay in the moderniza-tion of the society that might have been more speedily carried out had local rulers been disregarded. Indirect rule was a most con-servative policy, and when persisted in, as in Malaya and in some parts of Africa, it meant that when the British withdrew from Im-perial responsibilities, their heirs in authority were not a new and westernized class, but rather the old traditional ruling families, though admittedly many of these had had at least some immersion in Western ideas of government.

In general, all colonial governments, whether direct or indirect, tended to conform to the prevailing British conceptions of the proper duties and functions of government. They were to provide a system of law and order for the community, so that the ameliorative func-tions of European society might operate safely. They tried to keep out the influence of other colonial powers, collect enough revenue to sup-port themselves, and provide security for trade and missionary work.

This severely circumscribed idea of the proper role of government stemmed from a variety of sources: the traditions of limited govern-ment in Britain, the social and political disturbances aroused when government interfered too greatly in the existing ways of behavior of tribal societies, the costs of any program of social action, and the essential conservatism of the governing class. But increasingly the old traditions of laissez-faire, of limiting the responsibilities of colonial governments to the task of keeping the peace and maintaining stabil-ity for the operation of trade and Christian missions, became less acceptable. The emergence of nationalist agitation in many parts of the empire, and the attacks on colonialism throughout the world, put imperial administrations on trial and also on notice that the assump-tion of an enduring empire was doubtful.

Further, in Britain and throughout much of the rest of the world, the social functions of government were increasing; the responsibilities of the state for the welfare of those over whom it ruled grew greatly. All these trends were reflected in British colonial administration by the creation in 1929 of the Colonial Development Fund and in 1940, in the darkest days of the German blitz on London, by the Colonial Welfare and Development Act.

These creations marked a substantial change in the government of the British colonial empire. The competence of the public school and university graduate, however strong he may have been in character and leadership, to cope with all the multifarious problems of government was no longer accepted. Experts in many fields had to be assigned to deal with many of the graver problems of social development. The enactment of such laws also meant that one of the oldest shibboleths of imperial administration, that colonial governments could be best prepared for self-government by forcing them to be self-sufficient, was discarded. Under the new dispensation, such colonies were now to be aided in their growth. But all this meant much more management than had customarily existed; an active paternalism prevailed, and experts swarmed out from London to prod, poke, push, and otherwise help to drag some of the colonial people into the twentieth century. And the paradox of it all was that the colonial empire of Great Britain was perhaps never as closely governed as it was in the few years just before the essential dismemberment of the empire into the self-governing fragments that entered into the sisterhood of independent nations.

The paternalism of the period after the close of World War II survived the dismantling of Imperial authority, however. A colonial empire that had refused to subsidize its colonies when they were dependent because it might harm their initiative and spirit of independence showered them with subsidies after they were independent, and oddly enough, did this when Britain herself was beset with economic problems that set governments to tottering and had the British people living in a continuous atmosphere of financial crisis. And despite the financial difficulties of postwar Britain, the common criticism of British aid to its former colonies was that it was inadequate to their needs and that Britain should do more than she was currently doing.

During the closing decades of Imperial authority over the colonial empire, with the enlargement of the government's role in the social and economic life of the colonies and the consequent need for greater numbers of technical and administrative experts, there was an obvious need for the inclusion of larger numbers of native peoples in the ad-

ministrative structure. The civil services of the colonies were in need
of Africanization or Indianization, as the case might be. This need was
based on the demands of the colonial peoples and on the increasing
realization on the part of the British that the days of their authority
were numbered and that if they hoped to leave anything but chaos
behind them, they must prepare their subjects for self-government.

Of course, much that British rule had accomplished in previous
decades, when the prospect of the termination of Imperial authority
seemed so remote as to be impossible and when the British empire
seemed to have the fixed and enduring quality of a great mountain
range, had contributed, perhaps unconsciously, to the coming of
colonial independence. The establishment of peace among heretofore
warring peoples, the creation of a system of administration, of equal-
handed justice, of communication and transport, and of basic social
services, especially education, were all contributions that were paving
the way to the time when colonial peoples would demand the right
of self-government. But as this demand became more powerful and
British power drained away through the tragedies of war, it was
increasingly apparent that the only real question was whether British
withdrawal would leave anarchy or a going state behind it. Much of
the concern for the establishment of universities in the colonial world
and for the inclusion of indigenous peoples in the civil service was
based on the desire to leave stability rather than anarchy in the wake
of British departure.

The problem of the "nativization" of the civil service existed only
in the higher echelons of that service. Unskilled and semiskilled
posts had long been filled by the indigenous peoples, and the withdrawal of British authority would make no difference. But the almost
exclusively British personnel at the higher levels of administration
was one of the first and major sources of resentment when a class of
Western-educated natives developed and its members found themselves denied the opportunity for entry into government employment.

British colonial authorities started the process of the introduction
of non-Britons into the civil service in those Asian lands that had long
been under British rule. In Ceylon, for example, there were a number
of experiments devised in efforts to bring Ceylonese into the civil
service, but none of them met with much success, nor were they
pushed with any great vigor by British officials, and consequently the
number of Ceylonese in the service remained small. In 1920, however,
a new program designed to change the ethnic composition of the
service went into effect. This coupled with the establishment of a
University in Ceylon led to a large increase in the number of Cey-

lonese in the higher administrative apparatus of the island's government. British retirements and Ceylonese recruits worked their effects
until at the time of the establishment of the independence of the
state, less than ten per cent of the higher level civil servants of the
government were British.

Ceylon had made greater progress in staffing its service with natives
than had some of the other Asian areas of the British empire. In the
former India, that which was to become India and Pakistan, slightly
over fifty per cent of the elite positions in the Indian Civil Service
were still held by Britons at the time of independence in 1947. And in
Burma and Malaya, the proportion was still higher.

The reasons for the relatively slow pace in the Indianization of the
civil service in that land were numerous but never sufficient to placate
the educated Indian who had seen in his rigorously attained learning
the key to advancement in his country's service. Many influential
Britons who had served in India felt that Englishmen alone had the
upbringing, the education and character training, as well as the habits
of mind, the vigor, and the knowledge of the principles of government
essential for administration in India. This was a view scarcely likely
to meet with agreement from many Indians, but it was Englishmen
who were controlling the gates of admission to the higher levels of
Indian administration. There were other reasons adduced in support
of the British superiority for Indian administration. In the diversity
of races and creeds that formed the polyglot population of India, it
was the Briton alone who could stand aloof from the quarrels arising
from such divisions and guarantee a fair administration of justice and
the law.

In Africa, the pace of the local recruitment of civil servants was even
slower than it was in Asia. It was not until after World War II that
any appreciable strides were taken in this, though between the wars
it varied from colony to colony, and individual governors had appointed some educated Africans to administrative positions in the
1920's.

The nub of the argument in Chapters 1 and 2 is that the British
empire was created by power and maintained basically by the same
factor. This power was, of course, not best defined in absolute terms,
but rather in relation to the essential powerlessness of those Asians
and Africans whom the British encountered in the empire-building
process.

There were, however, practical limitations on the use of the power
the British possessed—many of them inherent in the political values,
ideas, and traditions held by the British themselves. And it was

pointed out that the true strength of empire existed in the productive power of the British people. The formal, discernible instruments of British power, the instruments of authority, were, like the visible part of the iceberg, but a small suggestion of the industrial, financial, and, to some degree, moral power that kept the empire both going and growing. This chapter is devoted, however, to that visible portion of British power—to the discernible apparatus of government and to the tools wielded by those in authority.

Supporting the somewhat diffuse system of civilian authority were "the armed forces of the Crown." This term covered all the forces raised and maintained by the government of the United Kingdom, the Indian government, and the governments of the Colonies, whether self-governing or dependent. But of course, the main forces were the British regular army, the Indian army, and the Royal Navy.

Compared with the armies of other European powers, the British army was a small and, in many respects, a peculiar establishment. The size and composition of the army reflected no coherent purpose or strategic consideration. In part this was due to the euphoric condition of nineteenth-century Britain in its relations with other powers. No other state was in a position to challenge Britain's worldwide preeminence. Secure behind the barriers of the English Channel and the North Sea, plus the vessels of the Navy, Britons felt a freedom from the perils of invasion available to no other people. Despite this, occasional waves of "invasion jitters" would sweep over the British mind. Various technological innovations bred fears that in some way or other the Channel had been bridged and the forces of France or some other state had a clear path to London if they wished to use it. Opposition to the Channel tunnel connecting Britain with the Continent was based largely on the fear that the security of Britain would thus be breached. There was a period in mid-century when the British, who of all people should have been most aware of the control the Royal Navy had over adjacent waters, gave way to their fears and put millions of pounds sterling and a good deal of faith in the idea that coastal fortresses provided a better defense for their shore than naval vessels. But these attacks of the jitters, these alarms of possible invasion were essentially irrational; the British people lived actually in greater security than any other European folk.

But if the army was not really necessary for the defense of Britain, what was it needed for? For many years, the act authorizing the maintenance of an army said that it was needed for preserving the balance of power in Europe. But in 1866, this was so out of accord with what appeared to be the realities of both European politics and British interests that the phrase was dropped. But what then was the purpose of the army? Unnecessary to the defense of the British Isles, apparently not required for support of the balance of power, the army, obviously, was needed for the defense of the frontiers of empire.

Certainly during most of the nineteenth century, the British army was mainly a colonial and Indian army. In the late 1860's, of the approximately one hundred and forty battalions in the army, about forty were stationed in the British Isles, some for the policing of Ireland, and the one hundred remaining were scattered throughout the empire, with the bulk of them serving in India. One critic complained that Britain had thrust an officer and a few soldiers into every nook of her colonial universe: "in every hole and corner we erect a fortification, build a barrack, or cram a storehouse full of perishable stores. . . ."[8]

Of course, this distribution of the army all over the British colonial empire gravely diminished its military effectiveness, save in small colonial wars. For any large-scale operation, the British army was disastrously ill-trained and ill-equipped, as the Crimean War in the 1850's showed so clearly and distressingly. The disasters that British arms encountered in such wars as the Crimean War and the later Boer War were certainly not due alone to the incompetence of military officers and commanders; much of the blame may be rightly ascribed to the political leadership of the state and, beyond that, to the essentially nonmilitary character of British society, and to its aristocratic bias.

During the greater part of the nineteenth century, the lot of the ordinary British soldier was miserable. It was expected that army recruits would be drawn from the lowest social classes in the British Isles, and that they could be held in line only by the toughest discipline. The soldier was regarded and treated "alternately as a criminal to be punished with flogging and as a child whose every action should be watched and guarded."[9] The term of enlistment was about twenty years, and the likelihood was that the bulk of that time would be spent outside the British Isles. Barrack living conditions were squalid and problems of sanitation and health neglected. The pay, of course, was miserly.

The revelations by newspaper correspondents of the neglect and mistreatment of the troops, and the general mismanagement of so many aspects of the war during the conflict in the Crimea, aroused a storm of protest and started a program of reform that gradually improved the lot of the soldier over the years. In addition, the idea of managerial efficiency in the direction of military affairs took hold and led to the abandonment of many traditional practices. Innumerable boards and commissions probed and prodded into the affairs of the army; victorious commanders of brisk little colonial wars captured the imagination of the British public and created interest in the army and its effectiveness. This process of reform was under way when the biggest of British colonial wars, that with the Boer South African republics, broke out at the close of the century. Boer victories in the early months of the war, and the long futile months of guerrilla war that followed against scattered Boer bands, indicated that there was much left to do. And then the emergence of Germany as a naval threat to Great Britain, and the growing military linkage with France added to the stimulus toward reform. This was carried out to such a degree that when war broke out in 1914, the British army, though miniscule in comparison with other major combatants, was perhaps the most highly skilled force in the struggle.

This British army, whatever the measure of its efficiency, was always a small force save during the years of major wars such as the two world wars. It was also a volunteer army, for Britain resorted to conscription only under the threat of world war, and then for as short a time as possible. Again, only in time of war did Britain draw heavily upon the manpower of the empire. The British army was British, recruited only in the British Isles.

The largest military force in the empire, other than the British army, was the Indian army. Here the principle of voluntary enlistment was adhered to even more stringently than in Britain itself; even during the crisis years of World Wars I and II, the Indian Army filled its ranks by voluntary enlistment. .

The Indian army was perhaps even more of a peculiar establishment than the regular British army. It was the instrument of an essentially alien government; a large proportion of its strength consisted of regular British regiments and specialist units serving in India, who were paid for out of the Indian budget while serving there. In addition, there were many more regiments and units recruited from the warrior elements of the Indian population. With the exception of the great Mutiny of 1857, and some lesser outbreaks before that, these Indian units served the interests of the British Crown with loyalty and efficiency. India was a great reservoir of strength for Britain in the lands east of Suez. Even as early as the Napoleonic Wars, Indian troops of the East India Company served in Egypt against France, and from that time on the participation of Indian troops was a normal feature of British wars not only along the borders of India, but also in Africa and in the lands to the east, such as Malaysia and China. And during the two world wars, Indian forces served with valor and distinction in many theaters of combat.

Indian troops were used in the Crimea in 1854–56, Persia in 1856–57, China in 1859–60, New Zealand in 1860–61, Ethiopia in 1867–68, Malaya in 1875, Malta in 1878, Afghanistan in 1878–81, Egypt in 1882, Sudan in 1885, Mombasa in East Africa in 1896, and in the Sudan again from 1896 to 1899. And less than a generation later came their extensive use in various theatres of war in World War I.[10]

While these Indian forces were a notable and invaluable addition to British strength, the Indian army during times of peace was not imposingly large. It usually numbered less than four hundred thousand men in all ranks, including the British regiments; the proportion of Indians to Britons ran about three to one. But it was a highly disciplined force, technically proficient, and well led. Of course, to Indian nationalists it was a basic tool of British oppression and a weapon used to deny their aspirations for self-government and independence. To British administrators, on the other hand, it was needed to protect the interests of India, not simply the interests of the British in India. But whatever purposes it served in its long career of warfare, the Indian army of British India was a notable source of strength to the British empire, and when Britain relinquished power in India and acknowledged the fact of Indian independence in 1947, the main support of British power in the eastern hemisphere disappeared. The old Indian army, now divided between India and Pakistan, served the national interests of the newly independent states. The former ambiguity of function disappeared, and with it disappeared much of British strength in that part of the world. By agreements with India, the British army continued to recruit Ghurkas, those sturdy and formidable warriors from the foothills of the Himalayas, but this was only a meager addition to British power compared to that which India had furnished in the halcyon days of empire.

In addition to the Indian army, Britain also established other forces recruited from the native populations of some of the colonial areas. There was at one time a West Indian Regiment that served imperial interests in various parts of the globe; there was also a West African Field Force. But although such groups were useful, they added little to the total military power of Britain.

Of much greater military significance were the contributions made by the major emergent nations of the empire, the senior dominions such as Canada, Australia, New Zealand, and South Africa, to the total strength and resources of the British empire both in World War I and the later conflict with Nazi Germany. It has been pointed out before, largely in relation to the Boer War, but is worth reemphasizing here that the contributions of these states to the war effort of the British empire were voluntary; the legions that formed in these states and marched to the battlefields of the world were created not by British command but by the decisions of their own democratic governments. There could be no more striking testimony to the meaning of the British connection in the lives of many of these people than the dimension of the sacrifice they made in the common cause in these wars. Inevitably, however, a sense of their own national identity began to outweigh their British attachments. This was especially true of those lands having large non-British elements in their population, such as Canada and South Africa. In some cause of common importance they might be allies of Britain once again, but the period of automatic rally and response to the needs of "the Motherland" were gone.

But as the waters of the globe are greater than the land, so was the Royal Navy greater in Imperial defense than the army; it was the most obvious and impressive of the elements of power of the nineteenth-century *Pax Brittanica*. But neither its prestige nor its predominance among the world's naval forces should obscure the fact that, like the British army, it had its oddities. Perhaps the most apparent of these was the general absence of strategic doctrine in the determination of its policies. Little if any attention was paid to theories of naval warfare; there was no organized study of naval doctrines. But then there seemed little occasion to study the art of naval warfare, for the omnipotence of British naval power was manifest. No European state was willing to devote the labor and capital to the construction of a navy sufficiently powerful to challenge Britain at sea, and British naval strength was generally maintained at a level thought sufficient for Britain to face a naval challenge from any two other powers and still have margin for safety. Despite this measure of security, there would be, as indicated above, occasional outbursts of hysteria regarding the alleged weaknesses of Britain's defenses, but these died down quickly in most cases, leaving the Royal Navy slumbering on in the "torpor of the long Victorian afternoon. . . ."[11]

The basic reason for this indifference to strategic planning was, of course, the lack of any real threat to British security. The naval force of Britain therefore was dispersed throughout the world, policing the waters of the world, and standing guard on the sea-frontiers of empire.

For these tasks, the Royal Navy developed a special type of craft that was for decades the most widely used and best-known embodiment of British naval power: the gunboat.

The gunboat was born during the Crimean War when a vessel was needed for operations against Russian fortifications in the narrow waters and shallow seas of the Baltic. But after that these small and lightly armored vessels were turned to a thousand and one uses on the world's waters, often participating in the Victorian mission of bringing law and order to "the lesser breeds without the law." The gunboats of the navy fought the slave traffic in Atlantic waters and off the east African coast. They tried to check the depredations of the "blackbirding" traffic (illegal recruiting or kidnapping of labor) in the Pacific. And the Admiralty entrusted to its gunboats the duty of the suppression of piracy off the coast of China and in Southeast Asia as well.

In addition to these duties, the gunboats were the chief instruments in the more agreeable business of "showing the flag," establishing the fact of British naval presence in many corners of the globe. This was carried out chiefly from the so-called "foreign stations" of the navy, stations that were, in fact, largely colonial in character. Many a harbor in colonial waters had frequent visits from naval vessels; others had such vessels constantly posted there. These vessels, and occasionally others of greater fighting power, were the visible embodiment of the links of empire; the white ensign they flew at their sterns was the visible sign of the protective power that Britain extended over the rights and interests of British subjects throughout the world.

But the use of the gunboat and the dispersal of British naval might throughout the globe depended on the acceptance by other great powers of British naval pre-eminence. The gunboats were a symbol of British naval might, not really an embodiment of it. Their fighting effectiveness was limited; they could, in the words of their leading critic, Admiral Sir "Jackie" Fisher, neither run nor fight. And when the sterner duties of protecting the sea lanes about the British Isles themselves from the challenge of the growing naval might of Germany arose, then the era of the gunboat and the associated dispersal of naval power throughout the globe had clearly come to a close. The gunboat era of the British navy yielded to the Dreadnought era; the small and lightly armed vessels that were the most obvious symbols of the pattern of "Law and Order" imposed by Britain and other European states upon the world gave place to the new fighting behemoths of the sea. These mighty vessels could indeed fight, but their very existence symbolized not law and order of any sort, but rather the essential anarchy of international relations that was to destroy the age of European hegemony.

A Britain concerned chiefly for the defense of its own shores, and also with the mounting costs of naval construction and maintenance, could no longer see any justification for the "frittering away" of its resources of money and naval manpower in a hundred and one varied duties around the globe when few of these duties seemed to have any relevance to British security. And so a vast reorganization of the British navy was started about 1903–4, under the prodding of the dynamic and abrasive Admiral Sir John "Jackie" Fisher. In effect, Fisher dragged the British navy out of the slumber of the late Victorian years into the harsh reality of German naval competition. He demanded the sacrifice of the gunboats and their ilk in the British navy and fathered the Dreadnought. And he concentrated British naval power in the waters close to the British Isles in order to meet the naval challenge of the Triple Alliance. This was not the end of British naval supremacy, though that too was to pass shortly after World War I; but it was the end of comparatively effortless British naval superiority and the end of the acquiescence of the rest of the world in the *Pax Britannica* which it sustained. Germany challenged that naval supremacy and failed, but it so weakened British naval strength, and Britain generally, that after World War I Britain had not only to abandon the two-power standard of naval superiority, but also to concede equality to the United States.

Perhaps the need to concentrate British naval strength to meet the German challenge was the first indication of the essential fragility of the British empire; even in the apparently halcyon days of greatest power, its naval strength had to take on an increasingly regional quality. Of course, this regionalism was not easily discerned. Britain had a worldwide system of naval bases, and the great virtue of sea power was the relative ease with which it could move about the globe. But when the British withdrew most of their sea power into the Mediterranean and North Atlantic waters, there were others who were ready to fill the power vacuums created by this new concentration. In the first decade of this century, the United States was building a navy that made it supreme in the Caribbean and the waters of the western Atlantic; in the Pacific, Japan was building on the naval victories it had won over China and was soon to demonstrate further prowess with the destruction of much of Russia's naval might in the Russo-Japanese war.

The British naval retreat from these areas was covered by the fact that Britain was diplomatically friendly with the United States and, after 1902, an ally of Japan. But the retreat was irreversible, and the costs and wastage of the great war of 1914–18 so huge that Britain never again grasped the trident of sea power with anything like the authority it had possessed in Queen Victoria's glorious days. And even if it had, perhaps sea power was no longer as important as it had been. Certainly the years following World War I saw the growth of air power to a position where its mobility and striking power seemed to outstrip those of sea power. To the demands of a great naval establishment were now added the costs of air power, and at a time when the resources of Britain in men, money, and morale were strained from the appalling costs of the first great war of the century. Air power might usefully take the place of manpower in patrolling and policing the frontiers of empire, in carrying out punitive raids against tribesmen beyond the frontiers of empire who were indifferent to the line between *meum* and *tuum,* but aside from small economies, the total costs of defense seemed more of a burden than many in Britain wished to carry.

These expenses might have been borne had Britain faced the postwar world in 1919 with efficient industry, a booming economy, and buoyant revenues. But unfortunately the reverse of all these conditions was true. The British industrial system, already somewhat outstripped by that of Germany and the United States before the war, was even further run down by the heavy demands imposed on it during the war. Britain, a nation that gained much of its living through world trade, found the traditional patterns of trade vastly disrupted by the war. And in its domestic market there was the mounting and persistent problem of unemployment, caused not simply by the disruption of trade but also by the generally obsolescent condition of equipment and techniques in many areas of British production.

Except for the growing relative weaknesses of British armed strength, the structure of power in Imperial Government did not seem to weaken. Indeed, in the colonies under Colonial Office government, and also in India, additional burdens of government were assumed as public opinion increasingly looked toward government for the performance of more social duties. But paradoxically, even as Britain was endeavoring to do a better job in the governing of the colonial peoples, even as she was abandoning the old principle that colonies should pay their own way in the world and was preparing to meet some of the costs of modernizing them, the world was increasingly coming to the opinion that good government was no substitute for self-government. A British empire brought into existence by British power, and sustained in large measure by the submissiveness or acquiescence of those it ruled, could not have much future when that power waned, and when there were increasing indications that the age of acquiescence had passed. Young men might still leave the dales of Yorkshire or the rolling countryside of Devon, might still go from the public schools or universities of Britain to serve as district officers or in any of several hundred other roles among the native populations of Asia and Africa, but they could not do it with the same sense of assurance as their predecessors. The great "European civil war" of 1914–18 had been too much of a shock for them to have quite the same faith in the virtues of European and British civilization. The war destroyed much of the "moral basis" of imperial authority, the sustaining sense of mission waned, and service in India or the colonies inevitably seemed less attractive. And as if the decline of British strength at home and the mounting resistance to Imperial authority in the colonies was not enough, there was the constant sniping at empire and imperialism from both liberal and communist sources. The Wilsonian creed of self-determination was abroad in the world, and from the centers of communist power came a constant stream of propaganda that, however distorted it was, found ready and eager reception in the minds of many.

Thus, in the words of Matthew Arnold, "the weary Titan staggered under the too great orb of its fate." The second great war, and the vast deterioration of British strength that followed it, meant the end of both the will and the means to sustain the burden of empire. As in earlier years Imperial power had withdrawn from colonies that were now the senior dominions and partners with Britain in the Commonwealth, now Imperial power was ended in India and the multifarious colonies of the Crown. This abdication of authority was made easier because of the existing precedents; India, Pakistan, Ghana, Kenya, and many other nations newly born assumed membership in the Commonwealth, and Britons found it easy to overlook their decline in authority because of Britain's senior membership in this worldwide grouping of states. And the withdrawal was done with grace. Seldom if ever has the burden of power been abandoned and a people emancipated from the weight of responsibility in such a creditable fashion. Occasionally there came a "knee-jerk" reaction to some event or disturbance abroad as if the days of Imperial grandeur still survived. The most notable of these was the Suez misadventure of 1956. Otherwise, though there was insufficient realization of what was going on, the structure of Imperial authority was dismantled with dignity. The process was complete for the most part by the mid-1960's. After more than one hundred and fifty years of operation, the Colonial Office wound up its affairs and retired from business. Britain was again a European state, as it had been in the days of Elizabeth I when the Imperial adventure began.

The

Economics

of Power

To trade with civilized men is infinitely
more profitable than to govern savages.

LORD MACAULAY

What is wanted for Uganda is what
Birmingham has got—an improvement
scheme. What we want is to give to this
country the means of communication by
a railway from the coast which would
bring to that population—which is more
intelligent than the ordinary populations
in the heart of Africa—our iron, and our
clothes, and our cotton, and even our
jewellery, because I believe the savages
are not at all insensible to the delights of
personal adornment.

JOSEPH CHAMBERLAIN

During the nineteenth century and much of the twentieth, Britain
had greater colonial responsibilities than any other power. Though
authority in local matters was increasingly transferred to the various
colonies, and though the prevailing concepts of laissez-faire limited
the role of government, the formal responsibilities of the Imperial
Government for the defense and security of British subjects and their
property throughout the globe were not substantially diminished. It

83

seems pertinent to inquire what enabled Britain to carry these responsibilities, and whether Britain gained or lost from the leadership of this great empire—in other words, to examine some aspects of the economics of the power she possessed.

A primary element, of course, was the fecundity of the British people. No state could possibly control, even in the formal and limited sense in which that word should be used, an empire as great as Britain's without the basic assets of vigor and growing resources. British population growth during the nineteenth century, though not spectacular, was substantial. In 1801, the first British census tabulated some 8,800,000 people living in England and Wales, with an additional 1,600,000 in Scotland. By 1851, the figures had grown to 17,900,000 and 2,900,000 respectively. By the close of the century they were 32,500,000 for England and Wales, and 4,475,000 for Scotland.[1] While a somewhat similar population increase occurred in many other states, the British Isles outstripped most, if not all, of the other European nations. Records of annual rates of population growth in European countries during the nineteenth century show that Britain was among the leaders in population increase during most of the decades of the century, and during some decades led all the states of Europe in rate of increase.

For many years the growth of the British population was generally attributed to the decrease in the death rate because of the improvement in health standards and medical facilities, rather than to a rise in the crude birth rate. This theory has been rejected in recent years, however, as incompatible with several acknowledged conditions of British society. For one thing, the increase in population growth was notable well before the most important of these medical advances, vaccination, was widely used. Further, the increase of population was just as great in those portions of the British Isles where medical facilities were almost nonexistent as it was in the more advanced regions. Recent investigations have tended to ascribe much of the increase directly to a higher birth rate. The causes of this rise are uncertain. Perhaps the erosion of the old patterns of rural society in the face of the growth of industrialization, and the subsequent drift of population to the towns, encouraged early marriage and a consequent increase in births. For the moment, the whole question is unresolved.

Whatever the causes of the increase in the population, that increase was substantial. It was a primary factor in British strength, both domestic and imperial, in the nineteenth century. Without this fecundity at home, Britain would not have been able to provide the migration that did so much to open up and people the frontiers of European

settlement. Not all of this migration went to the colonies; a great proportion of it went to the United States, but that proportion diminished
as the century wore on, so that by its close about 50 per cent of those
migrating from Britain were going, initially at least, to lands under
the British flag. In the hundred years between the battle of Waterloo
and the outbreak of World War I, over twenty million left the British
Isles to settle in countries outside of Europe. Thirteen million went to
the United States, four million to Canada (though what proportion of
these found their way south of the border is problematical), a million
and a half went to Australia and New Zealand, and a relative handful
to South Africa.[2]

It was a great outpouring of people, the greatest in British history.
In the decade 1843–52, it averaged annually about 214,000 persons; in
1881–90, 256,000, and in the first decade of the twentieth century, the
annual average of permanent departures from Britain was 284,000.
There were comparatively few entering Britain to take up residence
there, so that the inflow never came near to counterbalancing the considerable movement of Britons going abroad.[3]

It is easier to count the number of departing Britons than it is to
determine where they finally settled. As indicated above, it is difficult
to measure the flow of migration through Canada into the United
States and to isolate it from those who took up permanent homes in
Canada. But the problem need not concern us, for whatever the ultimate destination of those who left Britain, the flow itself is testimony
to the vitality and enterprise of the British people, to their willingness
to undertake the adventure of abandoning the old and familiar and
settling themselves in new lands.

Many of these lands were part of the empire, and the migration
tended to add new strength to the communities to which the migrants
moved and, in some measure, to add to the strength of the imperial
connection. But it was not invariably so. There were among the flow
of migrants many who left with a distaste, if not hatred, for things
British. This was most true of the Irish migrants, particularly those
driven abroad because of the devasting impact of the great Irish
famine of the 1840's. They carried anti-British feeling to the various
lands, imperial or not, to which they moved.

However useful and stimulating this British population growth may
have been to non-British lands by furnishing them with migrants, it
would have been an unmitigated disaster to Britain had it not been
accompanied by an even more rapid growth of productivity. Ireland
is the melancholy instance of the truth of this; there we see an economy whose production was stagnant while its population was expand-

ing, leaving the land so vulnerable that the attack of the potato blight in the 1840's brought on one of the worst famines and national disasters of nineteenth century European life. It was an awful example of what England might have been were it not for the spur that the Industrial Revolution applied to English productivity as a whole.

No country has ever industrialized in a painless manner, though the United States was more fortunate in this than most. Certainly the industrialization of Britain must have seemed to many Britons a most mixed blessing, if it could be called a blessing of any sort. The changes in agriculture that preceded the industrial age meant the expulsion of thousands from the soil and their subsequent drift into the towns. The emergence of new industries meant the enforced obsolescence of many of the old ways of production and the loss of trade and vested interest for those whose skills had been outmoded. The emphasis on thrift and the need for accumulation of capital meant the exertion of constant pressure on wages and the denial to the working class of all but the smallest possible share in the value of the goods they produced. But along with these unhappier aspects went greater economic expectations. Even though these advantages trickled down very slowly to the masses, they more than counterbalanced the burdens of industrialization.

Britain was the first of the world's nations to experience the grandeurs and miseries of industrial triumph. During much of the nineteenth century she held a monopoly on industrial power; not until 1870 did she seem to have serious rivalry. Before that date, Britain "was the very model of industrial excellence and achievement—for some, a pace setter to be copied and surpassed; for others, a superior economic power whose achievements rested on a special bounty of an uneven Providence, hence a rival to be envied and feared."[4]

Emulation of Britain's industrial achievements was for many European peoples the first order of business; it started early and continues down to the present, no longer in Europe, but in many of the non-European areas of the world. The hunger for the fruits of industry is world-wide, the desire for some of the self-sufficiency provided by industry equally widespread.

But in the years of the effective British industrial monopoly, Britons pressed to sell their goods to the rest of the world, and their customers lined up to buy. Nor was there much British tolerance for any "wantlessness" on the part of non-Europeans. Access to all the world's markets, even those that native rulers might wish to keep closed to the

rest of the world, seemed the natural right of a people who had un-
locked the gateways to a potential plenty and who were increasingly
persuaded that the manufacture and sale of the goods they produced
was essentially a duty, "the spreading of civilization" to those who
did not share in it.

Doors that were closed had to be opened to British sales; people
who might be wantless and unaware of the value of products of the
machine had to be brought within the ambit of trade. Africa, Japan,
China, all felt the pressure of British salesmanship, whether from eager
entrepreneur or from gunboat. Palmerston in 1841 said that it was the
government's business to "open and secure the roads for the merchant." And those who might wish to deny entry into their communities to British merchants and others, were to be compelled to
let them in. Just as the United States forced open the doors of Japan
for American and European traders, so Britain played the main part
in opening the doors of China.

The most powerful nation in the West, whose strength depended wholly
upon overseas trade and whose people were resolved to extend that trade
by every means, to push it with valour and to undergo hardships to carry it
to the ends of the earth, now pressed against the old closed market of China
and was resolved to break into it.[5]

But Britain did not have to force her way into most markets; the use
of force, as in the case of China, was rare. For the most part, the
world's customers were eager to take what Britain produced and to
sell what they could in British markets. The following table gives an
idea of the stupendous growth of British exports at representative
stages through the nineteenth and into the twentieth century.

1815	£	58,629,000
1855	£	116,691,000
1895	£	285,832,000
1912	£	598,961,000
1921	£	810,319,000[6]

The overwhelming bulk of these exports were manufactured products.
Coal was the only important raw material in the list of British exports.

Despite the vast sale of British products abroad, however, the
startling fact is that not once from 1822 to 1938 was there a single
year in which the value of Britain's exports exceeded the value of her
imports. Britain had a uniformly unfavorable balance of trade, buying

more goods, mostly food and raw materials, from the rest of the world than she sold.

This did not mean, however, that she was plunging recklessly further into debt with each passing year, for there were only three years from 1816 to 1913 in which the British economy did not enjoy a favorable balance of payments with the remainder of the world. This meant that British income from investments and from the sale of British services in brokerage, shipping, insurance, and banking more than outweighed the unfavorable balance of trade. It was not until the depression years of the 1930's that Britain showed a deficit on her over-all balance of current accounts with the rest of the world.

Up until the 1930's Britain accumulated through her favorable balance of payments considerable surpluses that allowed her to invest abroad in increasing amounts. Britain in the nineteenth century and in the first decades of the twentieth century was the banker of the world, the investment country *par excellence*. The flow of British capital into investment fields in other parts of the globe reached a tremendous scale in the first part of this century. If the same proportion of the American gross national product were devoted to foreign investments that Britain devoted in the fifty year period before the outbreak of war in 1914, American investments in other lands would have to come to between twelve and twenty billion dollars each year. No economy has ever placed such a large proportion of its capital funds in investments in other lands as Britain did in the late nineteenth and early twentieth centuries.

Britain slipped into the role of being the world's leading investment and banking state in the wake of the Napoleonic Wars. During the prolonged struggle against France, British wealth financed not only her own effort against Napoleon, but also much of that of her allies. The ironies of victory are apparent after every great war, and so it was in the post-Waterloo era. The public debt of France, the defeated state, was infinitely smaller than that of victorious Britain, but in part this was due to the greater maturity of the agencies of finance in Britain; the British had developed means of bringing the wealth of the community to the service of the state that far surpassed the methods used in France. And so in the postwar years, when France had to borrow to pay off some of the indemnity assessed against her by the victorious Allies, Britain and British banking houses provided a good part of the sources for the loan, and also the means of raising it. The firm principally involved was that of the Baring Brothers and their associates. This banking group became so important in the financial operations of postwar Europe that the French foreign minister, the Duc de

Richelieu, reportedly said "There are Six Powers in Europe, Great Britain, France, Russia, Austria, Prussia, and Baring Brothers."[7]

But areas other than Europe also floated loans on the British market in the same postwar decades. The Latin American republics, some of them still engaged in their struggle for independence from Spain, were able to secure credit from British investors for supplies for war or for their needs as independent states. And Britons who sympathized with the Greeks in their struggle for independence from Turkey also assisted in floating loans in the British market to aid the fighting Hellenes.

Something like a boom occurred on the London money market in the middle years of the 1820's, but like other booms, this one collapsed in disillusionment; South American mining ventures brought in little of the anticipated returns, and some of the states of the United States added to the gloom by defaulting on loans made by British investors. But despite these setbacks, Britain had taken long steps toward becoming the world's major financial power. Between 1815 and 1830, some fifty million pounds sterling had been lent to European governments, more than twenty million had gone to the less stable Latin American areas, and some five or six million more had been loaned to American states or invested in American business opportunities.

Many of the early experiences of British investors in lending to the United States turned out unhappily. Britons were most numerous among the many Europeans who owned stock in the second Bank of the United States,* and consequently suffered most severely from the Jacksonian war against the bank. And this was followed by the default of a number of American states on the loans they had contracted with British investment groups.

But any doldrums British investment activities may have drifted into were purely temporary, and in the 1840's there was a most remarkable revival of investment both at home and abroad. A key feature of this revival was the vast British interest in railroad construction, at first at home, and then later in numerous countries both in and outside the British empire. A second feature of the revival, and one of perhaps more enduring character, was the repeal of the Corn Laws, the adoption by Britain of a trade policy that meant the end of all restrictive or prohibitive practices in the control of trade and shipping—in a word, the adoption of free trade.

Whether a true world economic system was born in the nineteenth

---

* In 1841, out of the 350,000 shares of Bank stock, about 198,000 were held in Europe. Despite the fact that only American citizens had voting rights in the management of the Bank, critics of the institution made much of the alleged foreign influence in its affairs.[8]

century is debatable, but there can be little doubt that it came to maturity during that century, and that in the development of that maturity the British adoption of free trade played a central role. From the time of the adoption of free trade in the 1840's down through the remainder of the century, Britain threw its markets open to the rest of the world, imposing only a tariff for revenue on any imports. Britain became the world's greatest customer state, taking a vast proportion of the world's agricultural and raw material production. This abandonment of protection bore most heavily in the long run on British agriculture. Though the British landed interest remained powerful in British social and political life, the proportionate contribution of British agriculture to the total British national production declined, especially after the growth of the world transportation network made it easier to ship foodstuffs and raw materials from North and South America and the Australasian areas to British markets swiftly and at low cost.

But if the British landowner and farmer suffered by the repeal of the protective Corn Laws, the British manufacturer and investor—and much of the rest of the world—gained, for no enactment of any legislative body in the world contributed so greatly to the development of an economic cosmopolitanism as did the repeal of the British protective tariffs and restrictive navigation acts. With that repeal, Britons were free to buy what they would from the rest of the world, and the rest of the world moved to produce those products that they could sell in the British markets. Further, British investors were agreeable to the lending of their funds abroad, knowing that this hastened the production of goods that Britain needed and made it easier and cheaper to bring those products to market, and that there was no barrier to the free entry of these products in the British market. Thus British advantage was compatible with the welfare of the rest of the world.

The freeing of British economic activities from the restrictive trade and navigation laws came in conjunction with another development that contributed to the creation of a world-wide economy. This was the beginning of the nineteenth century boom in railroad construction, an activity in which British leadership, skill, and finance played a most important part.

The first commercial railroads powered by steam locomotives were developed in Britain, and Britain was the first nation to construct a national rail network. The first major boom in rail construction in Britain occurred during the 1840's; during that decade well over four thousand miles of track were laid, and soon after mid-century the major trunk lines of rail in the United Kingdom were laid down. During the years 1845 to 1850, one to two hundred thousand men were employed in Britain on railroad construction. This was a major economic drive, and required the mobilization of men and capital on a large scale; it was the greatest collective enterprise of Victorian Britain. The men who organized this effort were national figures and to some degree national heroes. Men with native ability, but without advantages of birth or inherited position, moved into the forefront of British life because of their leadership in railroad development and management.

This vast rail construction transformed many aspects of the British economy. One of the most significant changes was that a great many people who would rarely if ever have been pulled into the business of stock purchase or investment eagerly put their savings into rail company stock, as a "rail mania" swept over the British public. Something in the way of a "democratization" of the money market seems to have occurred, for few of the older firms of British finance entered into this boom; it was based on new men and new money, and on wider participation of the middle class in finance than had yet occurred in British financial history.

The interest of the British promoter, investor, engineer, and builder of rolling stock was not long limited to Britain; wider horizons beckoned, and soon Britons were involved in rail projects on the Continent and in North America. Before the close of the century there was no major part of the globe that had not felt the impact of British finance or enterprise in rail projects.

The great world boom in rail construction came in the closing decades of the century. From 1870 to 1913, the length of the rail network in the United States, Canada, India, Argentina, Australia, New Zealand, and Russia increased by over three hundred and fifty thousand miles. British finance took a large part in the construction of this vast rail network. Of course, its role varied from country to country, but the chief supplement to whatever could be mustered in the way of local capital and skill for rail development was the ability of developing lands to get support from the reservoir of funds and skill that had accumulated in Britain. Whether railroads were constructed by governments, by private companies, or by a mixture of both—perhaps the most common form of enterprise—there was at one stage or another likely to be an infusion of British capital or skill to initiate the enterprise or to spur it along.

Perhaps the influence of British capital in such activity was not always for the best. British investors were generally interested in rail projects that would open new areas of production for foodstuffs or raw materials that would ultimately find their way into the world economy or the British market. Wool from Australia, wheat and beef from Argentina and Canada, cotton from India and Egypt, such were the needs of the British market, and the railroads were frequently constructed in frontier lands in order to bring these imports as cheaply as possible to the British consumer. This could lead to a lack of balance in the development of the local economy, where productivity was controlled in some measure by the needs of the British market, and thus the economy was made satellite to that of Britain. But on the other hand there was the obvious need of many of these new economies to pay their own way in the world as quickly as possible, to produce a "staple" wanted by the rest of the world so that through its export they might purchase the other necessities for their own consumption. Further, there was the obvious economic benefit of specialization, of channeling labor and capital into the activities of greatest natural advantage.

Comparable with the growth of the world's network of railroads were the revolutionary changes in the world's shipping. Despite the importance of the rail systems, the oceans remained the great highways of commerce, and movement of goods over them was enormously facilitated by three major changes of the nineteenth century. First was the harnessing of steam power to navigation; second, the development of the screw propeller, replacing the sail and paddle wheel; and last, the adoption of the iron-hulled vessel. In all of these, British invention and enterprise played a part. By the close of the century, Britain had been the principal exploiter of the economic opportunities flowing from these changes. The size of the world's merchant fleet increased from nine million tons in 1850 to twenty million in 1880 and over thirty-four million in 1910; in this development Britain had the predominant place, so that at the outbreak of World War I vessels of British registry carried more than half the world's commerce and accounted for 42 per cent of the registered gross tonnage.[9]

Britain played only a small role in two of the major events speeding up the movement of world shipping. French capital and engineering skill created the Suez Canal, and American enterprise the Panama Canal. But the Suez Canal particularly was of very great significance to the British. It greatly shortened the route to India, the British bastion in the East, and also to some of the farther ports and lands beyond India, though the farther east, the smaller the advantage. Shortly after the opening of the canal in 1869, British tonnage formed about 75 per cent of the traffic through the new waterway. The canal also greatly stimulated British interest in the lands and waters adjacent, those areas through which shipping passed in approaching the canal. This strategic interest was substantially responsible for much of the later enlargement of British authority in Egypt and areas of East Africa.

Accompanying the greater facility in the transportation of goods throughout the world was greater speed in communication. American inventiveness had much to do with the development of the telegraph and cable system of the world. The United States was the chief beneficiary of a developing internal telegraph network; Britain gained the most from a system of telegraphic cables carrying messages under the world's seas. The first submarine cable connecting Britain to the Continent opened in 1851; Britain was linked with Calcutta in India by cable, not all submarine, by 1865. The following year Cyrus Field's long efforts to lay a trans-Atlantic cable succeeded. The cable system reached Australia in 1871 and New Zealand shortly afterwards. In much of this, Britain took the lead. While other nations also laid world-wide cable networks, in 1914 Britain was as supreme in this sphere as she was in shipping.

No statement of the factors that led to the creation of a world-wide system of exchange and to the mobility with which men, money, and materials moved so freely from one country to another would be complete without mentioning the widespread, indeed, the well-nigh universal adherence of all major trading nations to the gold standard. The British decision to open their domestic markets to the goods of the rest of the world under conditions of maximum freedom, the spread of the world's rail network, and the speeding up and growing efficiency of shipping services would never have made the contribution they did to the increase of trade had there not been general agreement on gold as the standard of value for carrying on exchange. Gold was the common currency of the trading world. To adhere to the gold standard was to be one with the civilized states of the world; to opt out of its use was to fall from grace. By the close of the century, every trading nation of any importance, with the exception of China, adhered to the gold exchange standard in international trade.

There were disadvantages to the use of gold as the basis of so much of international trading relations. Gold itself was a commodity, subject to fluctuations in production, fluctuations that were not always in amicable adjustment to the world's monetary needs. There were two major periods of plentiful gold production: the 1850's, following the

California and Australian gold strikes, and the 1890's, in the wake of the Yukon and South African discoveries. In the years between, the supply of gold did not keep pace with the expansion of trade and production, and many argued that this had a depressing effect on prices and contributed to the prolonged depression of the 1870's and 1880's. But such views generally had little acceptance in circles of orthodox finance; only in the United States did the question of the modification of the gold standard become a matter of great political controversy. The campaign of William Jennings Bryan in 1896, focusing on his advocacy of the use of silver as well as gold as a basis of currency issues, somewhat to the neglect of the international trade aspects of the matter, was perhaps the major manifestation of dissatisfaction with the gold standard. And even that faded out after the flow of gold from the gold rushes of the Klondike and South Africa began to be felt in the monetary system of the world. The gold standard won yet another major adherent in 1897 when Russia adopted it.

All of the factors so far discussed—the willingness of Britain to be a great importer of raw materials and foodstuffs and exporter of capital, the shrinking of distances through technological change, the speeding up of communication, the common use of gold as a convenient method of settling the balances of payments between nations in their trade relations and as a means of giving acceptability to currencies throughout the world—created a complex, intimate, and relatively frictionless system of world trade. And in that the British economy was very close to being the prime mover. Chief supplier to the world of goods, marketing and brokerage services, shipping and communication facilities, and loans for development in frontier communities, British merchants, bankers, and officials presided over a financial system of infinite complexity and sophistication that constituted an "empire of trade." This empire was more important to Britain than the empire of territory that was colored red on the maps. And the two empires were not coterminous. The profits of the empire of trade and investment made possible much of the improved standard of living within the British Isles, and only in part did these profits come from the lands clustered under the British Crown.

As has been indicated above, the value of British exports rarely exceeded the value of imports; Britain habitually ran a deficit on her balance of trade. The deficit on British trade had varied greatly from year to year throughout the century, but it began to rise sharply after 1872. It first reached one hundred million pounds in 1876, and skyrocketed to one hundred and forty-two million the next year. For the next twenty years it fluctuated between ninety and one hundred and twenty million pounds. Then another period of growth in the trade deficit developed. It reached its apex in 1903, when Britain paid out one hundred and eighty-eight million pounds more for the goods she bought than she received for the goods she sold.

Towards the close of the century there was an increasing concern in some British trade circles about this unfavorable balance of trade. Some business men and politicians advocated the creation of a form of Imperial trading union in which British goods would have tariff advantages in colonial markets in return for comparable advantages for colonial products in the British. This Imperial preference would mean the forsaking of the free-trade policy that Britain had followed for half a century or more. But despite the outcry, Britain remained true to the free-trade faith, and throughout those parts that Britain ruled directly there were no barriers erected against the goods of other nations, just as there were none in Britain itself. Legally the colonial territories ruled by Britain had open doors for the traders and investors of any nation. Practically, of course, the British trader and investor had numerous advantages over foreigners when competing for markets in British territory. Common language, greater and easier credit facilities, a natural predilection to do business with one's own, all worked in Britain's favor, even though no conscious policy of exclusion or discrimination against foreigners prevailed. And indeed, any idea that Britain would have gained by trying to build a wall about its own and Imperial markets seems odd. She had no need to do this, as is clear from the trade figures of the time. During the period from 1854 to 1913, about 73 per cent of Britain's trade was with foreign countries, and only 27 per cent with the empire.

Those foreign countries with whom Britain traded, however, and who might all be regarded as part of the British trading empire, were generally among the less developed of the world's areas. They were primary-producing states, trading their products of farm, field, and mine for British industrial products. Thus Britain became accustomed to concentrating its trade not upon the empire, but upon the primary-producing lands. And on the whole, these were not the markets with the highest growth potential, nor was trade with such lands likely to bring out the greatest competitive effort or highest technical skill of British industry. Such markets were essentially too "soft" and easy; Britain's command of, and concentration upon such markets left it less fit to cope with the more competitive economic world of the mid-twentieth century. This, perhaps, is not the least of the costs of former Imperial greatness.

The alarm over the unfavorable balance of trade, and the related agitation for "fair trade" took little account of the fact that Britain was still accumulating wealth through what have been called "invisible exports." These were the revenues from shipping, banking and insurance, brokerage, and other services that Britain rendered to the international economy. Returns from British investments formed an increasing proportion of these "invisible exports"; Britain was more and more living on her creditor function in the world. Increasingly under challenge in the markets of the world by new industrial nations, she depended more and more on the vitality of her loans and investments abroad to pay her way in the world and increase her gross national wealth. There was no year from 1891 to 1906 in which Britain did not have to depend on the income from overseas investments to keep her out of the red in her international accounts.

This shift in the nature of Britain's income was one of the background factors in the adumbration of the idea of the imperialism of finance capitalism, that theory of imperialism, referred to in Chapter II, whose most notable exponents were John A. Hobson and the leader of the Communist revolution in Russia, Vladimir Ilyich Lenin.

The roots of this theory of capitalist imperialism are of a diverse character; some of them lie in the body of classic European doctrine and theory of the nineteenth century. But it was less these intellectual roots than the fact of the rapid expansion of the territories under the British and other European flags that led John A. Hobson, a British socialist, to the writing of his important tract, *Imperialism*. The fact that British capital invested abroad represented an increasingly important element of the total wealth of the United Kingdom, that more of British national income was coming from these investments while the income from trade was growing much less rapidly, shed "clear light upon the economic forces which are dominating our policy."[10]

What Hobson called the "taproot" of this new aspect of imperialism was the inability of consumption to keep pace with the growth of production; maldistribution of consuming power prevented the absorption of commodities and profitable use of capital within Britain. Surplus capital could not find effective employment at home and was driven to look abroad for opportunities for return. "It is not too much to say that the modern foreign policy of Great Britain is primarily a struggle for profitable markets of investment. . . ."[11] But it was not Britain alone that Hobson indicted; other advanced industrial states such as France, Germany, the United States, and Holland were all controlled by the same forces within their own economies.*

---

* In fairness one must note that Hobson somewhat modified his views in later editions of *Imperialism*. His views became more flexible and less deterministic, and his indictment against capitalism as a breeder of wars and empires became an indictment against certain capitalists only.

Lenin took up this particular thesis in the midst of World War I and gave it further development in his own work, *Imperialism, the Highest Stage of Capitalism,* published in 1916. It was soon to become an established part of the Communist creed, profoundly affecting the Communist view of the world. It influenced, if it did not control, the foreign policy of Communist states, and generally brutalized and debased the interchanges of diplomacy between Communist and non-Communist states because of the Communist adherence to the simplistic equation: Capitalist = imperialist = war monger.

But not only Communists have been influenced by the Hobson-Leninist theory. Western secularized peoples, sensitive to the economic forces within their societies and accepting the concept of "economic man," have been vulnerable to the Leninist thesis, especially because of its monistic and simplistic character. It has thus become deeply embedded in the public mind of many non-Communist peoples. Unfortunately, its acceptance exceeds its validity; it has become one of the controlling myths of the modern world.

Critical examination of the thesis reveals that from its very inception coincidence was taken as evidence supporting the theory. There *was* a marked enlargement of empire at the close of the nineteenth century; the British and other nations *did* engage in what became known as the "scramble for Africa." And at the same time there was an accumulation of capital seeking investment opportunities in foreign and colonial areas. Much of Hobson's evidence consisted of throwing these two factors together and then drawing what was to him an obvious conclusion from them. Of course, Hobson did not have access to official documents. Now that these are open, they reveal that the overwhelming interests of British officialdom were defensive and political, not expansive and economic. But a relevant and available fact to which he paid no heed was that British money was not flowing and did not flow into the areas of recent or prospective annexation. It continued to go into the areas that investors had always found attractive: the United States, Canada, Australia, New Zealand. Within the empire the "old empire" was much more appealing than the "new," and the tropical empire inhabited by non-Europeans received a pitiably small share of British funds at the very time when such funds were most available to the world. On the average, less than twenty million pounds per year went to those tropical areas that today constitute the largest proportion of the so-called underdeveloped regions of the world. India, Egypt, and what is now Malaysia seem to have received together less than ten million pounds each year of British investment funds.

The reasons for this are not difficult to find. There was political stability in the colonies of European settlement that did not exist in tribal societies; there were entrepreneurial classes and skilled labor that could be brought speedily into the processes of sophisticated production; there were local markets of substantial buying power that made investment for industrial production reasonably profitable.

Another objection to the Hobson-Leninist thesis is that it assumes that the state is always the obsequious servant of the finance-capital elements of the society. This view of the state, of government as the tool of the "ruling classes," is of course a dogma deeply embedded in the *corpus* of Marxian faith, as deeply as that of finance-capital imperialism. How close this theory comes to the realities of political power in late nineteenth century Britain is highly debatable, but few students of British Imperial policy are inclined to give it great credence. Certainly British politicians were sensitive to the concern of British industrialists and merchants for the widening of markets and were occasionally willing to use diplomatic and military power in order to pave the way for the entry of British goods into markets that would otherwise have been closed. The instance of China has already been cited; from the same period of exuberant diplomacy one can also cite the efforts of the British government to open the Ottoman Empire and its satellite state, Egypt, to European and especially British trade. And in the next decade or so, the British government supported British traders in their ventures on some of the rivers of West Africa. But this was free-trade imperialism, demonstrating a desire to enlarge the sphere of British trade rather than to extend the territorial empire for the benefit of financial interests.

The idea of bending the forces of empire for the profit of financiers was likely to be remote from many of the men of government. Neither of the major political parties in Britain was particularly eager to serve the needs of the investing community. In the ranks of the Liberals there survived a good deal of the mid-century faith in free trade as a means of rescuing mankind from the evils of war and imperialism, and a deep suspicion of all forms of activity abroad other than that which sought the advance of quiet trade and Christian missions. Gladstone, who left the stamp of his powerful personality on many members of the party, was the personification of this tradition, and while there were Liberals who worshipped at other shrines and "knew not Joseph," the Gladstonian tradition was too powerful to allow the party to snap to attention at the behest of bankers and other financiers.

As for the Conservatives, they were perhaps no more willing to use the apparatus of power, the armed forces of the state, for Imperial interests; at any rate their identification of such interests would certainly not give pride of place to wider opportunities for investors. There was too much of the old tradition of land-holding aristocracy enshrined in the party for it to be susceptible to "pushy" interests arising from the City, the financial heartland of the nation. There was also an uglier aspect to this latent hostility to some of the financial community, and that was the undercurrent of anti-Semitism in British life at the time. It was not as blatant as it was on the Continent— Britain had no Dreyfus case, nor did Britons produce anything akin to the notorious *Protocols of the Elders of Zion*—but there was a hostility to Jews among the ranks of the radicals because they were associated with banking and finance, and among clubland Conservatives because they were regarded as assertive, sometimes vulgar, and in general, in the English phrase, "too clever by half." Much of this latent hostility came into the open during the Boer War, when opponents of that war were quick to give a prominent place to Jewish bankers and financiers as instigators of the struggle.

At the time when Hobson wrote, Africa was the area in which British territorial expansion was going forward most briskly; this expansion and the war in South Africa furnished Hobson with much of the material of his argument. But the most recent substantial scholarly work on British policy in Africa during the late nineteenth century indicates strongly that the things that mattered to British officials directing British policy in that part of the world were strategic and essentially defensive in character.

It was largely concerned with defending the maturing inheritance of the mid-Victorian imperialism of free trade, not with opening fresh fields of substantial importance to the economy. Whereas the earlier Victorians could afford to concentrate on the extension of free trade, their successors were compelled to look above all to the preservation of what they held, since they were coming to suspect that Britain's power was not what it once had been. The early Victorians had been playing from strength. The supremacy they had built in the world had been the work of confidence and faith in the future. The African empire of their successors was the product of fear lest this great heritage should be lost in the time of troubles ahead.[12]

The same concern for defense is revealed in the words of a former British Prime Minister in 1918, commenting on British interests in the making of the post-World War I peace settlement:

Every time I come to a discussion—at intervals of, say, five years—I find there is a new sphere which we have got to guard, which is supposed to protect the gateways to India. Those gateways are getting farther and farther from India.[13]

   To regard the Hobson-Leninist thesis with skepticism and to accept that idea that late nineteenth-century British Imperial expansion was somewhat old-fashioned and essentially defensive in motivation does not, of course, mean there were no economic interests or concerns in empire and its enlargement. It means rather that such interests were infinitely more diversified in character than Hobson and others suggested. One does not throw the thesis out the front door only to have it return through the back in the statement that there were some British investors who found profit in investments in newly acquired lands in Africa. But there were also merchants who found new markets opening to them in such areas, and there were administrators, soldiers, seamen, and professional men of varying stripe who also found indirect economic advantage in the enlargement of empire. Economic motive there is aplenty, but no "taproot" of expansion, rather still the same forces of expansion: industrial power, a quickening of communications, a cheapening of the cost of carrying bulk goods, a widening demand for raw materials in Europe, and a growing desire for the products of Europe throughout the world, justified by the sense of civilizing mission with which so many Europeans approached the non-European world.

   What then did this tidal wave of influence, goods, and funds moving abroad from England and from other countries do to the lands over which it spread? What was its effect on the receiving societies? To a great degree the answers are as varied as these lands themselves, for the effect of investment depended greatly on the capacity of the peoples to respond to it—their capacity to use it or to have it use them.

   For example, two contrasting responses to the impact of modernity upon ancient societies are found in the differing reactions of neighboring Asian peoples, China and Japan, to the enforced opening of their doors to European and American entry. In the first case, the ancient Chinese way of life broke under the strains and the tension set up by increasing pressure of the Western world upon it; in the other, the Japanese had sufficient resiliency and adaptability to be able to absorb Western industrialization without overthrowing the established hierarchy of Japanese life.

   Perhaps the main difference between the two societies is to be found in their differing attitudes toward the outside world. The Chinese long nourished the faith that China was the only true civilization and that all non-Chinese were essentially barbarians and tributaries to the Son of Heaven. One of the most notable expressions of this attitude was the Chinese Imperial response to British trade and diplomatic emissaries of the eighteenth century. The Chinese felt that Britons had nothing that China could possibly need, but they would be allowed limited admission, provided always that the merchants behaved themselves. Otherwise the trade would cease and Britain would be brought to her knees by the Chinese denial to her of such necessities as tea and rhubarb.

The shock of learning that the Confucian values and the threatened embargo on tea were insufficient to protect China against the intrusion of the West, notably during the wars with Great Britain, led to a growing tension within Chinese society; the last effort of the old Chinese order to hang on to power and maintain some sense of its own adequacy occurred in the so-called Boxer Rebellion of 1900. With its defeat by a combination of forces from European states and the United States, the road was barred for a return to the ancient virtues. Modernization in some form was essential, but the way to achieve it remained unclear even in the late 1960s, as the Cultural Revolution in the ranks of the Chinese Communist state revealed.

Japan, on the other hand, while having an embryonic nationalism and a hierarchical social order, was in less of an intellectual strait jacket. There was a greater readiness to grapple with the fact that Japan had fallen behind other states within her wall of isolation, and therefore a much greater readiness to respond to the challenge of Western impact by vigorous re-ordering of her own life. The Japanese worked wholeheartedly to transform their agrarian feudal society into an industrial state and achieved their objective without the assistance of foreign capital. Perhaps the most ironic aspect of the contrast between these Asian peoples was that in 1895 Japan defeated China in a naval war fought with European-type men-of-war; while the vessels were similar, the men and officers of the Japanese fleet revealed an ability to adjust to modern naval technology unknown to the Chinese. And Japanese army units were a large part of the relief forces that came to the aid of Europeans and others penned up in Peking during the Boxer uprising.

To a great degree then, the effect of British trade and investment in various parts of the world depended on the reactions of the local society to the impact of the Western ideas and technology that came in the wake of British influence and funds. The most efficient and sophisticated of these responses naturally came from those lands peopled by European migrants and their descendants. Europeans who had migrated to Canada, Australia, South Africa, and other lands carried in their intellectual baggage the entrepreneurial spirit and a receptivity to modern technology. Such populations contained among them men who were alert to the possibilities of the machine and modern industry and were eager to share in the benefits and profits flowing from them. These local entrepreneurs were the eager local allies of investors from overseas who put money into the local economy. There seems no reason to quarrel with the belief of Adam Smith that new countries settled by Europeans advance "more rapidly to wealth and greatness than any other human society."[14]

But entrepreneurial classes did not exist in all societies, or if they did they were not numerous enough or skilled enough to take advantage of the flow of European investments. And in some cases, the manner in which the investments were handled by the British barred the way to any effective local share in the development of modern industry. India is a case in point.

The British invested rather heavily in India during the nineteenth century. By 1913, about 10 per cent of British overseas investments were in India; the amount was something close to $1,800,000,000, There were innumerable advantages to India from this flood of investments; the capital was made available at cheap rates between 3 and 4 per cent, and with it the British government in India constructed what economists call the "infrastructure" necessary for modern industrial growth: the railroads, highways, telegraphs, port facilities. In addition, the British presence there impcsed on India the widest measure of internal peace and stability in its modern history. But despite this large flow of investment funds and the introduction of many of the attributes of the modern state into India by the British, India did not derive full advantage from these factors. In part, both India and Britain were to blame for this.

Hinduism is the faith of the majority of the Indian people. The abiding and controlling values of this faith are renunciation, asceticism, and a belief in the essentially illusory character of the material world. As a major Indian scholar has put it:

Eastern civilizations are interested not so much in improving the actual conditions as in making the best of this imperfect world, in developing the qualities of cheerfulness and contentment, patience and endurance. They are not happy in the prospect of combat. To desire little, to quench the eternal fires, has been their aim.[15]

All of which amounts to an admirable prescription for economic stagnation, however rich the spiritual rewards for such asceticism.

Of course, this does not mean that all Hindus embrace renunciation with fervor; many fall short of such high religious ideals. In addition, Hinduism is an exceedingly inclusive faith; its cheek to cheek mingling of the severest austerity and the grossest sensuality has been remarked upon ever since Europeans first began to comment on things Indian. So in Hinduism there has always been ample place for those who sought the values of this world rather than those of the next; men who bought and sold, who manufactured and traded, all with an eye for profit, were numerous among the Indian population. There was no lack of a potential entrepreneurial response to the flow of investment funds from abroad, even though many aspects of the society worked against such a response. It must be remembered that when Europeans first landed in India, it was one of the great productive societies of the world. Bengal, the first major area to fall under British control, had a successful textile industry.

What India did lack was men with knowledge of modern industry. The British were not ruling a society that was ripe for modern industrial development, a society that was only waiting for the touch of the Aaron's rod of investment to have great gushers of production flow forth, refreshing the land. Rather, "They imposed themselves on a society for which every index of performance suggests the level of technical, economic and administrative performance of Europe five hundred years earlier."[16]

The British did introduce modern technology into India, and in other ways laid the groundwork for the later development of industry. This was, of course, a tremendous achievement, but much of it was done without any concern for encouraging the development of a modern business community. This was in part the result of policy, of the lack of awareness of the problem, and a dogmatic faith that the economic creeds that suited British needs were equally applicable and efficacious in India.

The British role in India has frequently been described as that of "guardians," guardians of the peace and the general welfare of the people. But effective government requires more than guardianship. If there is to be a fundamental change in the life of the people, if they are to be involved with and enlisted in the great task of the modernization of their society, there must be a close identification between rulers and ruled. In India there is grave doubt as to whether the British wished to modernize or westernize Indian society. The great Mutiny in 1857 had revealed the dangers involved in seeming to attack established Indian values too heavily; there were also many Britons, so-called "orientalists," who questioned the efficacy of grafting Western ways onto the deeply rooted tree of Asian life. The general trend of British policy was to seek collaborators for its rule among the leaders of the existing order of society rather than among those who would be the instruments of change—among the princes, rajahs, *talukdars*, *sirdars*, and other traditional figures, rather than among the industrialists of Bombay.

Further, in an age of increasing nationalism, any close identification between rulers and ruled became more difficult. Previous conquerors of India, and the land had known many in its long history, had been assimilated into Indian life, but the roots of the Britons were still in the British Isles. Despite years of devoted labor and service that many gave to India and its people, India was not, and never could be "Home." The fact that British investments in India did not stimulate the growth of Indian industry as greatly as an equal sum of Indian investments would have done stems a good deal from this situation. But the fault was not purely a British one; Indian enterprise was lagging.

British initiative and investment flow in India was, as suggested above, largely directed toward equipping India with basic facilities rather than with manufacturing plants, power resources, or extractive industries. The chief British investment interest was in railroads; through British action India had the most extensive rail network in Asia. But in their construction of these arteries, the British did little to stimulate the growth of Indian industry. India turned to Britain for virtually all the materials for rail construction and operation; locomotives, rolling stock, rails, signalling equipment, and other products were all secured from British manufacturers. This would have been necessary in the initial stages even had the planning and construction been in Indian hands, but no native government would have been as indifferent to the development of local industries for the supplying of their wants as the British were.

Part of this indifference to the encouragement of Indian industry stemmed from the prevailing acceptance of laissez-faire economics by British governments both at home and in India. Laissez-faire, of which British free-trade policies were one of the most important expressions, did much to create the great world economic order of the nineteenth century. But it also had a tendency to condemn colonial areas to be the hewers of wood and the drawers of water, to limit them to providing the industrial states of Europe with raw materials and foodstuffs, while in exchange Europeans turned out the finished products with the widest measure of freedom. Sir Charles Trevelyan,

Finance Member of the Indian Government in the 1860's, reflected all this when he wrote:

> . . . looking at the great advantage England has in cheap capital, cheap coal, cheap freight & the indescribable facilities arising from its vast and varied mechanical arrangements, I do not think that any Indian . . . manufacture can stand the competition. . . . Agriculture must be its great staple industry. . . .[17]

That laissez-faire, however, would not only stimulate maximum productivity, but that the resultant commercial exchange would tie the nations of the world together in the collaborative arrangements of peaceful trade, seemed an admirable idea to even the most anti-imperialist Britons. To Richard Cobden, for instance, certainly no friend of the empire, free trade was "God's diplomacy, and there is no other certain way of uniting people in bonds of peace."[18] The merchandise that left British shores, he felt, carried the seeds of intelligence and productivity to the less-enlightened. Such doctrines furnished all the rationalization necessary to condone an indifference to the encouragement of Indian industries. And lack of positive action to aid such growth under the existing circumstances condemned India in many ways as severely as if the old eighteenth century system of mercantilist restrictions still prevailed in Imperial policy. Indian tariffs, for example, where they existed at all, were confined to a level that furnished revenue but no protection. Of course, lest this indictment seem too severe, it must be recalled that for much of the nineteenth century India had a favorable balance of trade with Britain; she exported more raw materials than she imported manufactured goods, and she took payment for the difference in large amounts of silver bullion that drained much of that metal out of the world's monetary system. Further, this Indian silver was not invested productively, but went into jewelry and articles of personal adornment which were of little economic use.

But the British unwillingness to impose tariffs where they might have encouraged Indian industry was but one facet of their whole attitude toward the problem of governing India. For there came to exist what might be called a post-Mutiny syndrome, which made them hesitate to cope with Indian problems for fear of arousing rebellion. Essentially only a government strong either in the support of its people or in its dictatorial control over them is able to impose upon a society the costs of industrialization, and the British government in

India had neither such support nor such control. It was timid, fearful of arousing opposition, reluctant even to tax sufficiently, and it justified these attitudes through the prevailing economic concepts of laissez-faire and hostility to active government fostering of economic growth.

Yet despite it all, an Indian business middle class, adjusted to the modern industrial world, gradually emerged. That the weight of the prevalent religious faith was a handicap is suggested by the fact that the first signs of the new entrepreneurship appeared among non-Hindus who had lived long in India but were not fully in the mainstream of Indian life. The Parsees near Bombay, descendants of migrants to India from Persia many centuries before, and a people who had maintained their religious identity apart from Hinduism over the intervening centuries, were the first to enter into the world of modern industrial technology, but they were joined by other non-Hindu groups such as Jews and Armenians. While some Hindus joined the small business communities in India during the nineteenth century, it was not until the development of a strong nationalistic movement with an emphasis on the development and use of Indian products that they began to participate in modern business activity in any numbers. And even then, some of their participation was influenced by the Gandhian rejection of the machine in favor of the old-fashioned spinning wheel.

Gandhi, the leader in the movement for Indian independence, was strongly opposed to industrialization in his land. In 1938 he was still staunchly standing by views that he had first expressed thirty years before:

It was not that we did not know how to invent machinery, but our forefathers knew that, if we set our hearts after such things, we would become slaves and lose our moral fiber. They, therefore, after due deliberation, decided that we should only do what we could with our hands and feet.[19]

As time passed, the British government in India slowly yielded its laissez-faire principle and began to take more positive action for the development of Indian industry. A strong-willed Viceroy, Lord Curzon, set up a Commerce and Industry Department with the duty of aiding provincial governments in the promotion of technical education and industrial development. But World War I brought the real change, and the government accepted the idea that it had to play an active part in the promotion of Indian industry. The most notable, though not the only change, was the adoption of protective tariffs for a number of industries. With this more positive attitude came a substantial growth of Indian manufactures and the increasing ownership and employment of Indians in managerial roles in the economy. The British, however, still retained the major position in the Indian economy even down to the years immediately following Indian independence.

Despite all of the limitations of British policy, India benefited from its association with Britain in many ways not suggested here. Britain was the agency through which Western influences reached the Indian economy, and while her presence and policies in India laid burdens on that people, the gains for India outweighed these costs.

Not all would agree with this judgment, however. Indian nationalists have, with varying degrees of fervency, made much of the so-called "drain" Britain imposed on India as explanation for India's poverty and lack of effective modern development. The "drain" arose from various charges imposed on India by British rule: charges for public indebtedness, for the maintenance of military forces greater than India required and useful mostly for the protection of British interests, for the salaries paid to Britons for services that Indians should have been performing, for the pensions paid to them when they had finished their labors and retired to Cheltenham or Bournemouth in England, there to live comfortably on the taxes paid by the sweating Indian peasant and laborer. The litany of such charges was lengthy, and constituted a large part of the Indian nationalist indictment of British rule in India. This drain, it was alleged, deprived India of capital that might otherwise have gone to the development of Indian industry, so that India, instead of benefiting by the availability of British capital for investment purposes, was actually being drained of capital because of British rule in India. The cheap loans were nothing but India's capital returning to India, and being used for purposes not always in India's highest interest.

Of course, British historians and economists have not accepted the charges without rebuttal. But in any such argument one is soon confronted with the difficulties of weighing the general peace, unity, and order that prevailed in India during the period of British power as against the specific charges on that land's economy. The argument seems sterile; the economic relationship between Britain and India over the centuries is simply one aspect of a vast complex of emotional intangibles, and the whole can never really be effectively measured. Britain can reasonably be criticized for many faults in India, but since her departure it seems increasingly apparent that the end of

British rule did not solve as many problems as the nationalists expected; the more serious of them still exist in the traditional values and
institutions of the society.

The total British impact on India suggests the substantial limitations
on the degree to which an alien ruler can modernize or revolutionize
a colonial society. Compared to the vigor of the Japanese response to
Western ideas, the Anglo-Indian response seems rather flabby. The
industrialization of Japan was brought about almost entirely by native
enterprise and has notably been vastly more effective than that of
India.

. . . until the end of the nineteenth century India was well ahead of Japan
in the volume of manufacturing production. This was mainly owing to the
relatively early development of her cotton and jute industries. During the
first decade of the new century the gap between the countries was narrowed,
and after about 1910 Japan drew ahead. From then on her advance was
much faster than India's. By 1937 the index for manufacturing production for
Japan was 550 and 240 for India (base year 1913 for each country), and
Japan then turned out a volume of industrial output nearly three times as
great as India's.[20]

Whatever the inferences that may be drawn from this contrast, it is
clear that however substantial may be the contributions made by
others, whether rulers or not, there is no substitute for native initiative
and enterprise. India did not provide a congenial environment for the
growth of a native industrial society; the blame for this is essentially
India's, but the British must take their share.

In many of the British dominated areas of Southeast Asia, the British
encountered an entrepreneurial class already in existence, though not
one composed of the native peoples, but rather of Chinese migrants
into the regions. This was most true of Malaya. The major sources of
wealth in that area have come from tin mining and rubber. In the
1870's, when Britain took over the political direction of the various
states of the Malay Peninsula, the Chinese were already masters of the
tin mining of the region and had been so for some decades. They
brought habits of hard work and enterprise into the business that
virtually eliminated the native Malays from it; they also brought *tong*
and civil wars into the area, and thus contributed to the British
intervention and pacification. There can be no doubt, however, of
their entrepreneurial skill, and the Chinese dominated tin mining
until 1929, when European capital using dredge mining gained an
ascendancy. Smelting of tin also required greater capital outlay than

the Chinese mining interest could muster, and European, largely British, capital created that aspect of the business.

Out of the substantial returns from tin mining came the revenue for the construction of railroads in Malaya, so in this case it was British initiative more than capital that counted. The rail mileage in Malaya was miniscule compared to that of India, but it opened up large areas of agricultural land in which the rubber plantations so important to the total Malayan economy were later to emerge.

Native South American products had a great impact on Malayan economic development. Coffee flourished as one of the main crops in Malaya for the period from about 1885 to 1905, but by the latter date coffee culture was virtually extinct in Malaya and agricultural interests were turning eagerly to another import from South America, rubber.

The British were responsible for a scientific introduction of rubber cultivation in Malaya and for much of the development of the rubber plantation system. But they were not alone in the expansion of this product on the peninsula; capital from India and from Malaya itself contributed to the swift development of rubber growth in the area. Malayan rubber speedily established its superiority over that of South America. The great rubber boom along the banks of the Amazon died out, leaving some rather grandiose towns founded on its wealth to languish and die while the range of rubber plantations throughout Malaya increased rapidly. Despite the later competition created by the development of synthetic rubber industries in the advanced countries of the West, rubber remained the backbone of Malayan exports, sharing the spotlight only with the long-standing export of tin.

The very grave dependence on one or two cash crops evident in the Malayan situation is the basis of a common indictment against the use of European investments in colonial economies; it is also part of the criticism previously made of the lackluster efforts of the British in hastening the industrialization of India. "By stressing exports of raw materials and discouraging industrialization while leaving noncommercial agriculture in a state of 'static expansion,' colonial policy throughout the nineteenth century facilitated a lop-sided development."[21] So runs the tenor of an extremely familiar complaint about the results of European investments in colonial lands. There is much truth in the statement, but as it stands, it is too strong. In India, as suggested above, the true charge against the British was not that they discouraged the growth of Indian industries, save perhaps that of textiles, but rather that they took little action, and that only belatedly, to encourage such development.

But whatever the degree of British failure in this matter, it must be remembered that economies dependent on one or two exports for their purchases from the rest of the world have been a common feature of the world's economic patterns ever since the development of some form of international trade; they were not the simple creation of European imperialism. Medieval Britain was largely dependent on the sale of her wool abroad, long before the age of European expansion and the development of the capitalistic order of affairs. Nearly all communities have relied on a staple product to tie them to a market abroad or to a larger economic order during the early stages of their economic growth. Virginia depended on tobacco during the American colonial period, and the southern states of the American union on cotton as their nexus with the world of trade. Australia relied on wool, Canada on timber and wheat, New Zealand on dairy produce, Argentina on beef, Brazil on rubber and then coffee, Ghana on cocoa, Malaya on tin and rubber, and such a list might still be extended.

This phase of economic development has occurred so universally in the history of economic growth, both before and after the age of European hegemony, and in societies that were colonial and non-colonial, that to attribute it to a colonial relationship alone is surely a distortion. Countries wishing to have access to the goods and services produced by other societies have to pay for them, and the readiest form of payment lies in their production of the goods that can be grown or obtained most easily and cheaply, and which find acceptance in other lands. Scarce capital will flow rather naturally to those activities that bring the greatest return; it is possible to divert capital and labor to other activities, but not without the risk of lowering the annual productivity and impairing the rate of growth as a whole. The new society must grow a surplus of a commodity that can find markets abroad; the surplus buys the necessities for development in other types of production, i.e. capital, machinery, labor possessing the needed skills. Independence from this need for production and sale of surplus, this concentration on a staple or two, can be bought, but only at the price of the enforced diversion of labor and capital into less productive economic activities.

But the point of the discussion is that economic dependency is not confined to colonial economies, but is essentially a natural stage in the process of economic growth. Political methods may be and have been used with varying degrees of success to hasten progress through this stage, but if forced draft efforts are made, the results are frequently disastrous. The recent economic histories of Ghana and Indonesia testify to that.

The economic experiments conducted by such states as Ghana and Indonesia, however disastrous they may have turned out to be, are indicative of the drift of the world away from the nineteenth century faith in laissez-faire. But the fact that many states and peoples have departed from the laissez-faire creed should not blind us today to the remarkable achievements of the economic world order of the nineteenth century for which it furnished the theoretical underpinning. Under the instructions of the great classical economists from Adam Smith on, the British led much of the remainder of the world in the abolition of restrictions and regulations that limited the range of economic opportunity for many; they opened the doors to a world of freedom for men to migrate in search of better markets in which to sell their labor or of a greater chance to deploy their skills. Closely accompanying them in this was the accumulation of British capital, paving the way for the establishment of new industries that served British markets for agricultural products and other raw materials, but also bringing non-European peoples into the world economic system and helping bridge the gap between the countries where the modern industrial age was born and those to whom such modern industry was alien.

But with the passage of years, the social ideals of western European states condemned the doctrines of laissez-faire as inadequate for human needs. The positive functions of the state were enlarged in pursuit of social justice. In British colonial administration this led to the adoption of the Colonial Development Act of 1929, and the later Colonial Welfare and Development Act of 1940. Under the terms of this act the government of the United Kingdom pledged itself to make free grants to colonial regions of the empire for research, education, industrial development, and a variety of other causes. In the wake of the financial and other strains left over from the war, the program was somewhat slow in getting under way, but from 1945 to 1955, some eighty-five million pounds were spent on such projects, and the rate of planned expenditure was set to increase to one hundred and twenty million pounds for the five years from 1955 to 1960.

This legislation and the programs of colonial development created by it marked a significant change in the general British policy that colonies, with rare exceptions, should pay their own way in the world. But whether the new paternalism or the older "sink or swim" attitude was the better preparation for the nationhood that was being increasingly demanded by colonial peoples is unclear at this writing.

The new paternalism, however, was part of a new age of positive government. The old laissez-faire days of the nineteenth century were gone, and with them the economic cosmopolitanism and free movement of goods and men that they had allowed. Nationalism, sometimes of the most chauvinistic and even xenophobic type, ruled men's minds; the world economic order that Britain had done so much to create, and which was in so many ways the true British empire, was disappearing, battered by the shock of two great wars, vitiated by Britain's increasing economic weaknesses, and challenged by the new age of national economic planning and controls.

5

The
Arrogance
of Power

The English in India are the representatives of a belligerent civilisation.

SIR JAMES STEPHEN

Coloured races should be treated with every kindness and affection, as brothers, not—as, alas, Englishmen too often do. . . .

QUEEN VICTORIA

To extract that which is uniquely British from the general story of racial and cultural confrontations due to the expansion of Europe is a difficult, indeed almost impossible task. The whole story of such contacts is a lurid and brutal one, illuminated by brighter flashes of understanding, compassion, and concern for others. The general doctrine of the legal equality of all subjects of the Crown permeated the administration of justice in the British empire, but the realities often fell short of this noble ideal.

During the first years after the establishment of British power in portions of India, notably Bengal, relations between Britons and Indians certainly betrayed little racial antagonism. Many centuries of foreign rule had destroyed any political and national awareness that the Hindus of Bengal might ever have possessed; the British were nothing more than another in a long line of conquerors and alien rulers, and they were not likely to encounter much native opposition as long as they left Hindu customs and religious practices undisturbed. Indeed to many the British were preferable to the Muslim rulers who had attempted forcible conversions among the Hindus and had discriminated against them in a variety of ways.

Some of the earlier British rulers in India actually felt that they had much to learn from their recently conquered subjects. The first of the great British proconsuls in India was Warren Hastings. Wise, moderate, and essentially sympathetic in his dealings with Hindu men of learning, he was able to gain their confidence and they disclosed much of their ancient learning to him. Thinking Englishmen such as Hastings and Sir William Jones found much to enjoy in their contacts with Indian society. And even for the nonthinking there was generally little segregation. Military victories and consequent prestige gave British officers entry into Indian aristocratic society; friendships between Britons and Indians were not uncommon, and business collaboration was frequent. There was apparently little racial tension or sense of superiority on the part of either Britons or Indians in their dealings with each other.

This happy picture, however, was not to last. A social gulf between Britons and Indians appeared and grew wider. The rift was due in part to the changes in British government in India. The days of casual ease and corruption following the British triumphs at arms in the eighteenth century disappeared with the establishment and growth of a government with a grave sense of its responsibilities. The governor who started the new era of attempted incorruptibility was Lord Cornwallis, a British aristocrat. It was his opinion that every "native of Hindustan, I verily believe, is corrupt."[1] The only way to purge the government of corruption was to remove all natives from the higher governing positions. In this simple faith and practice, government did become more honest, but also much further removed from the people. Contact with the leaders of native society was diminished as government became more austere; separation of the two races became more apparent.

Then too, the high positions of British authority in India were increasingly filled by aristocrats, and those who were accustomed to the haughty manner and olympian air of command when dealing with their own people were not likely to become companionable and democratic when dealing with Indians. Increasingly the English in India knew Indians only as servants, a situation disastrous to any real understanding between the races. As one Englishwoman remarked in 1810, "Every Briton appears to pride himself on being outrageously a John Bull."[2]

This whole trend toward cultural arrogance and isolation received powerful reinforcement with the famous decision that English would be the language of learning and education in India. The adoption of this policy, associated with the famous state paper of the historian, Lord Macaulay, was close to inevitable. It was natural that the language of the conquerors and rulers should prevail, as, for example, Norman French had been the language of the court and barons in England after the Norman Conquest. Further, there were manifest advantages for India in having the wider contact with the European world that even an enforced knowledge of British would bring. The languages of India are so diverse that almost a generation after the establishment of Indian independence, the governments and people of India had not effectively made a decision about the official language of the state. But all the advantages that the wider knowledge of English would bring to India and its people could not entirely excuse the brusque and casual manner in which Macaulay thrust aside the native tongues; he called them "poor and rude" and proclaimed that one shelf of books in English was worth a whole library in Sanskrit. It was not a sentiment with which such men as Warren Hastings and Sir William Jones would have agreed, nor was it a sentiment that truly reflected Macaulay's genuine concern for India and its people.

Of course one result of the decision was an increasing isolation of the British rulers from the ruled. In a caste-ridden society, the British became another caste. With English the official language, Britons sent to India had less incentive to learn the tongues and the ways of the people they ruled. The more energetic, able, and dedicated of them, of course, learned the languages they needed and sought to find out all they could about India, but despite these efforts they increasingly formed a type of mandarin class. A distinguished British jurist in India, Chief Justice of the province of Bombay, said of his fellow Britons about the middle of the century:

The Chief administrators of our vast Indian Empire are so completely severed from the bulk of the population, by colour, race, language, religion, and material interests, that they are often, if not habitually, in complete ignorance of the most patent facts occurring around them.[3]

In a few years, the outburst of the Indian Mutiny gave startling substance to these opinions.

Scholarship added to the alienation between the ruling caste of Britons and their Indian subjects. The unfortunate story of the influence of James Mill and his *History of British India,* published in 1818, has been suggested earlier. As a Utilitarian, with a general contempt for many of the traditional and established values in all societies, Mill thought that Hinduism was an obscurantist set of beliefs totally out of harmony with enlightened thought. Unlike Warren Hastings and Jones, Mill could see little to admire in Indian life. Arguing essentially from the fact of the relative ease of the British conquest of India, Mill said of the Indian people that:

Their laws and institutions are adapted to the very state of society which those who visit them now behold, such as could neither begin, nor exist, under any other than one of the rudest and weakest states of the human mind.[4]

Because they were a conquered people, they and their culture must be inferior. "In truth, the Hindu like the Eunuch, excels in the qualities of a slave."[5] Mill's assumption that because the English had found India in a divided and distracted condition it had always been that way was pure ignorance, but it was an ignorance shared by most other Britons and also by many Indians. Even an Englishman more sympathetic to the Indians than Mill could write in 1841, "The most prominent vice of the Hindus is want of veracity, in which they outdo most nations even of the East."[6] Such works were used in both English and Indian universities and formed part of the general course of study for young Englishmen wishing to enter a career in the Indian Civil Service. This type of instruction for young Englishmen was bad enough, in that it lent an academic gloss to the prejudices and parochialism many already possessed. But perhaps it was even more damaging in the case of the young Indian, for it meant to him the loss of part of the heritage of his society and the diminution of his own self-esteem; he was being trained and educated to fit his condition of political inferiority.

In extenuation of the work of these British historians, it can be stated that there were few if any Indians to teach them better. Indians had very little knowledge of their own past and indeed very little concern about history as process at all; they were not a historically conscious people. The limited work done by men such as Sir William Jones and other Europeans had reached a wider audience in Europe than it had in India, and it was not until the latter half of the nineteenth century that the labors of European scholars, British among them, managed to bring to light the evidence on which today we form our opinions of the antiquity and achievements of Indian society prior to the coming of European hegemony.

The views promulgated by European scholars that the forefathers of the Hindus belonged to the same group of mankind from which were derived all the nations of Europe famous in ancient and modern times; that the Vedas, the sacred literature of the Hindus, were the oldest literary works in the world; that the Upanishads contained the most profound philosophical speculations that the human mind has ever conceived; that the Emperor Asoka united the whole India and Afghanistan under one rule . . . and that, thanks mainly to his efforts, Buddhism, originating in India, played a great role in civilising a large portion of the population of the world, so much so, that even today one-fifth of the human race still profess that faith;—all these could not fail to stir deeply the hearts of the Hindus with the result that they were imbued with a spirit of nationalism and ardent patriotism.[7]

This is the modern and sounder view of India's past, and it is a view to which British scholars have made many contributions. But it is something quite new, and when the nineteenth century British historians wrote of the Indian past, they simply read what they knew of India's eighteenth century confusion and nineteenth century subordinate status into all the past of that land.

To the older and dismal view of Indian history was added the impact of the missionary and evangelical impulse on the European mind in the shaping of a view of Indian life and culture. There had been a time when Englishmen going to India left their women in England and their religion at the Cape. India had an abundance of both women and religions, though Englishmen took more readily to the former than to the latter. The East India Company, intent as it had been on peaceful trade, and concerned to avoid troubles, had tried to bar missionaries from entering India, fearing that their proseletyzing efforts might arouse Indian antagonism. But the Christian zeal that emerged in eighteenth and early nineteenth century British life was not to be denied. All the new missionary societies established in England during the closing decade of the century wished to open up the Indian mission field; they mobilized opinion in Britain behind their demand, and in the revision of the charter of the East India Company in 1813 Parliament accepted a clause that stated "that it is the duty of this country to promote the interests and happiness of the native inhabitants of the British dominions in India, and that such measures ought to be adopted as may tend to the introduction among them of useful knowledge, and of religious and moral improvement. That, in furtherance of the above objects, sufficient facilities shall be afforded by law to persons desirous of going to and remaining in India for the purpose of accomplishing these benevolent designs."

The statement of intent was clear, but the check rein was still applied to missionaries; they were admitted only under license, and they could not acquire land nor establish a permanent settlement. These restrictions were ended in the next charter revision in 1833, however, and from then on missionaries were allowed to operate in India with only those restrictions that generally applied to all subjects of the crown.

An attitude of unfriendliness to missions was common in government circles in India for many years. Such opposition, however, was small in contrast with the general resistance of the Indian people encountered by the missionaries. Many Indians felt that the missionary societies were the cultural arm of British authority. As one Indian remarked to a pioneer missionary: "You English have taken the whole country, and now you want the people to receive your religion. They would be great fools if they did." To such resisters the whole missionary endeavor was essentially a form of cultural imperialism. Indian religious culture has assimilated many creeds and practices through her long history, but an alien faith of essentially exclusivist character —"Thou shalt have no other gods before Me"—that came apparently arm-in-arm with foreign rulers was bound to be viewed with suspicion.

But "by their fruits ye shall know them," and in many cases the fruits of missionary labor were admirable. Encouragement of education, support of literature, attacks on practices that, however much accepted by Hindu tradition, could not be regarded as other than a violation of natural law and decency—all these activities testify to the honest efforts on the part of the missionaries to elevate the standards of Indian society. They attacked infanticide, the practice of *sati* (the immolation of widows on their husbands' funeral pyres), the self-infliction of torture as a form of religious testimony, and other practices they found repugnant.

Since the missionaries were dependent on voluntary contributions in Britain for the maintenance of their work, however, it was in their interest to demonstrate the need for their presence and activity in India. One way to do this was to paint Indian life and religious practice in the darkest hues; this would give them their greatest justification and would most affect potential contributors. In addition, most of the major missionary societies published journals in which the work of the missions was widely disseminated, and thus the British public's

concept of India was shaped by the missionaries' tales of Indian im-
mortality and "barbarism."

The humanitarian efforts of the missionaries could not disguise or
excuse the fact that to many Indians, they were, as much as the
military officers of the Crown or other employees of the state, agents
of the conquering power; they represented more the spirit of British
authority than they did the spirit of Christ. Despite the advice of one
of the earliest English missionaries in India, William Carey, that the
missionary should be as "one of the companions and equals of the
people to whom he is sent,"[8] the cultural shock of the Indian environment was too great for many of them, and they, like their nonmis-
sionary compatriots, retreated into the sanctuary of a pattern of living
that was as English as they could make it. This naturally deprived
them of contact with the people, their country, and their customs.
Such alienation led easily to lack of understanding and appreciation
of the richness of Indian culture, and what they did not understand
many were ready to condemn. Some early Baptist missionaries, for
example, were sweeping in their condemnation of Indian music as
"heathen" and "disgusting," something that far too easily brought to
mind "practices dishonourable to God & ruinous for the soul."[9]

Under the conditions, then, in which Christianity came to India,
not in a vacuum, but associated with British power and personified
by men who, with some choice exceptions, were reluctant to admit
their all too human failings, it is natural that many Asians saw it not
as the opportunity to share in a faith and belief of inestimable value,
but rather as an imposition from outside. It was a tragic element in
the history of the Christian missions that this association was almost
inescapable, and it was observable not only in India, but in Africa and
other areas of great missionary activity.

It is paradoxical that it was some of the better impulses of British
life and administration that most disturbed Anglo-Indian relations.
The purge of corruption and the creation of an honest administration
were admirable, but the price paid was the elimination of many
Indians from the employment of the East India Company and its
government. The missionaries went to India with the intent of making
available to the Indian millions the "good news" of Christianity, of
sharing with them what they felt was the greatest gift that Western
society could give them, the gift of Christian grace. But with it all
there was the implied attack on Indian ways, the rejection of much
that the Indian thought to be equally holy, and the alienation of the
Indians from their European rulers. So, too, with the coming of the

wives of the Englishmen to India, the gain in family morality and stability was notable, but the price was yet further isolation of the Englishman in India.

Few Englishmen ever took wives to India during the eighteenth century. Most who went were young men in search of fortune who could not afford marriage had they the inclination. Further, an Indian career was fraught with danger. The voyage to India was long and hazardous; once there the perils of life were grave. The absence of English women led to concubinage with Indians: England and India met in bed. But with the passage of time and the consolidation of British power in India, some of the insecurities diminished, though they never vanished entirely. Women arrived in greater numbers; the practice of concubinage diminished, and the keeping of harems or "zananas" declined. The number of European women in the English establishment increased slowly, however; in 1809 there was apparently one female to three males, and under these conditions the continuation of the illicit relations between Indian women and Britons continued for some time. But the coming of the missionaries and of the women transformed English society in India, both for good and ill.

The most obvious of the unfortunate results was the greater tendency of the English community to retreat to ever more tight little social circles, from which nearly all Indians were excluded, and in which the Englishwomen often took over the role of the guardian of the family and community against the weaknesses of the wandering male and the assumed lack of virtue of the Indian female. Little outright physical cruelty was involved in this, rather the casual contempt that has so often marred relations between Europeans and other peoples during the years of empire. Children picked up and repeated the shop-worn terms of abuse employed by their parents in speaking of Indians: "odious blacks," "nasty, filthy creatures," "black vermin" were some of the terms in common use.

The tendency to try to live in a European enclave, meeting Indians only as servants, was reinforced by a fear that Indian males somehow found European women almost irresistably attractive. To Victorians it was a "well known fact" that darker races were physically more attracted to Europeans than vice versa. This was a myth that persisted despite the considerable evidence to the contrary. And adding to all this parochialism and prejudice and to the sense of arrogance manifested by many Western people in their dealings with Asians and others was the development of nineteenth century pseudo-scientific doctrines of racial differences and gradations.

The development of doctrines of racial differentiation and the belief in the existence of superior and inferior races have a long and tangled history. The essential simplicity of the origin of man as recounted in the Book of Genesis, the notion of the whole human race being the descendants of one male and one female, made for the unity of mankind. Such differences as existed were ascribable to disruptive events such as the Flood and the scattering of peoples after the abandonment of the Tower of Babel. It was, therefore, easy for most to accept the equality of men as did Dr. Benjamin Rush, American patriot and friend of Thomas Jefferson, when he stated, "The history of the creation of man and of the relation of our species to each other by birth, which is recorded in the Old Testament, is the . . . strongest argument that can be used in favor of the original and natural equality of all mankind."[10] This acceptance of basic equality among the races was grounded on acknowledgment of the scriptures and of Christian revelation. Not all would accept this doctrine of equality; David Hume, the Scottish philosopher and historian, commenting on what to him seemed to be the failure of the Negro people to produce eminent scholars, men of letters, or warriors, held that "Such a uniform and constant difference could not happen, in so many countries and ages, if nature had not made an original distinction betwixt these breeds of man."[11] Hume was an atheist and thus regarded the biblical mythology with scorn. But he was too ready with a judgment based on ignorance, for neither he nor anyone else knew anything about the history of the Negro nor of Africa.

The general attitude typified by Rush was supported by a sentimental idealization of non-European peoples with whom the Western world was becoming familiar. The early reports of the great voyages of Captain Cook in the Pacific in the 1770's made many familiar with the people of the South Seas. Cook and his companions reported them to be amiable and hospitable, possessing natural virtues untouched by the corrupting influences of Western life. True, they were excessively inclined to petty theft, but it was done without malice; the Maoris of New Zealand practised cannibalism, but, in compensation, they were brave and manly. When Cook returned from one of his voyages with a Pacific Islander named Omai, the latter became the petted darling of London society, and the leading magazine rhapsodized over the primitive virtues, "But what signifies the mind's being vacant, if the heart be full, and the sweet emotions of nature agitate it."[12]

This splendidly sentimental and patronizing view harmonized in many respects with the missionary ideas that the non-European peoples in many parts of the globe possessed a sweet simplicity of mind that would make them easy converts, and that in the "sweet emotions of nature" the seeds of Christian faith could be easily planted. But little of this applied to India; the whole idea was more suitable for the Africans and the people of the South Pacific Islands. The Indians had too complex a religious faith, and the missionaries felt that the Indians were not ruled by "sweet emotions" but rather by an infinitely complex set of rules and relationships, most of which seemed to the English grounded in superstition, mysticism, legendary nonsense, and ritual. It was impossible for most of the English missionaries to realise that their eating of beef from the cow sacred to the Hindus, or their indifference to the elaborate system of caste was as morally offensive to the Hindu as temple prostitution or the practice of *sati*, never very widespread, was to the Christian.

It was natural that Europeans in the midst of Asian peoples and in other exotic surroundings and cultures should ask questions: From what does the difference between us and them come? How is it that we have the power to command and they the duty to obey? To an earnest Christian such as Charles Grant, one of the early British officers in India, the questions presented no problem. If the Englishman ruled in India and was in so many ways manifestly superior to the Indian, the African, or any of the other numerous native peoples over whom he ruled, it was because the English had for centuries benefited from the enlightened and ennobling influence of the Christian faith. From this it followed that God had chosen "His Englishmen" for the transformation of India into a more seemly and spiritual society.[13] To Grant and other earnest Christians, it was the will of God or the decree of Providence, but while there might seem an immutable quality about this, what God had decreed, God could change. Once that task had been accomplished, then the sanction was ended and the British day in India closed.

Other Britons would more likely simply assume that the general superiority of European, and most especially British, civilization accounted for the power Britain had in India. Of the various aspects of that civilization, many would place Christianity first, thus agreeing with Grant; others might stress material progress, scientific advance, naval and military prowess, industrial might, or any and all of them in some combination. With all of such explanations there was an element of hope that sooner or later India might be brought to the same level of civilization, for all of these analyses of British triumphs and conquest were based on social or cultural considerations, and few were willing to admit in that day of social progress that India and Indians were ineducable. Indians could learn to emulate their masters, and with that and their conversion to Christianity, there would be no essential difference between Britons and their subjects. Thus Macaulay looked to the day when England would have created in India a class of persons, Indian in blood and colour, "but English in tastes, in opinions, in morals and intellect."[14]

Perhaps the explanation for British power that was most likely to justify a permanent British *raj* in India was the notion that British power in India was based on some special characteristics of the British people or, in the more popular language of the day, on the unique qualities of the Anglo-Saxon race. The social and cultural conditions that seemed to explain British ascendancy might be changed by the forces of education and imitation; the mandate to bring enlightenment to the Indians might be withdrawn by the Providence that had entrusted it to the British; but the possibility of the changing of the race and the loss of the peculiar virtues of the Anglo-Saxons was remoter than either of these other possibilities.

Theories of race pervaded a great deal of the social thinking of the later nineteenth century. The facts of physical differences among the peoples of the world had led to efforts to classify those people into major categories or races, and to arrange them in order of intelligence or power of moral perception. Whatever the general criteria of such classifications, if done by Europeans they all had a most satisfying tendency to place the European or Caucasian at the top of the ladder, and then to rank other peoples in varying orders beneath them. But this was not done with any real display of scientific knowledge and was generally associated with a realization that race was only one of a number of factors that had caused the differentiation of one group from another.

It was not until the latter part of the century that race became not just *an* explanation, but rather *the* explanation of the differences between people, and of the "superiority" of the Europeans. Much of the new authority for racialist interpretations of history came from the publication and wide acceptance of Charles Darwin's *Origin of Species* in 1859. A great deal of the pre-Darwinian thought had been devoted to the classification of species, races of man amongst them, so much so that Darwin's great work came not as a new revelation in the history of thought, but rather as the great synthesis. It swept the intellectual and scientific world almost without opposition, for it represented an idea whose time had come for fulfillment. And in the doctrine of natural selection, vulgarized in a sense into the idea of the survival of the fittest, many found the real explanation of the ascendancy of Europeans, and particularly Britons, over the Asian and African peoples. "Dominion over palm and pine," it seemed, was not the result of the accidents of history, but rather of the immutable laws of biological and human progress. In effect, what we can recognize today as the results of the accidents of history were to many of the latter-day imperialists in Britain, and to much of the Victorian world, the fruits of the essential process of natural selection and development. Might made right; Imperial power carried its own justifications, and the English would remain in India and elsewhere by virtue of the racial superiority of the Anglo-Saxon over the lesser breeds of mankind. The human kingdom was like the animal kingdom: the strong took from the weak and the intelligent from the strong.

The new racialism received reinforcement with regard to India by the events of the great Mutiny there in 1857, two years before the publication of Darwin's work. Britons in India had a sense of betrayal from the uprising; atrocities on both sides widened the already broad gap between the British and the Indians and left the former ever more distrustful of the latter. One scholar says of the post-Mutiny period,

Almost without realizing it, the British threw over the whole notion of Indian regeneration and consigned the Indian people to the status of permanent racial inferiority. . . . Their only hope lay in the long-continued rule of a beneficent British government.[15]

Much of the late nineteenth century racialism is reflected in the writings of that bard of empire, Rudyard Kipling. There can be little doubt that Kipling had a genuine fondness for India; this is most apparent in *Kim,* perhaps the most mature of his Indian stories. Kipling also was fond of some Indians, though this affection was felt only for the servant class: the regimental water carrier, Gunga-Din, for example, and those other servants who looked up to their English masters with reverential obedience. The faithful servant, the dutiful soldier, these are likely to be the quasi-heroic figures in most literature written by rulers about their subjects; so it was with Kipling. And the other side of the coin is equally true: the educated Indian, the university graduate who might compete in the entry exam of the Indian Civil Service or challenge in one way or another the exclusive right of the British to rule, was the object of Kipling's condemnation. Thus, the short story "Head of the District" records the abysmal failure of the Indian, Grish Chunder De, to succeed in the ruling of a district in India, despite his success in the entry exams, his travel abroad, and the general fact of being "more English than the English." For despite all these excellent virtues, he still lacked the important quality of race; fate had denied to him the excellences given only to Anglo-Saxons.

It has been charged that Kipling sold himself to the British governing class, not financially, but emotionally, and was a salesman for the empire. It is perhaps too harsh a charge. Kipling was born into that governing class in India; almost every Englishman of any importance in India belonged to it, and Kipling's father had an important educational and artistic position in India. In extolling the virtues of the Anglo-Indian governing class, and the virtues of the lowly who served them with devotion, Kipling was simply expressing the values of the class to which he was born, and few of that class in India were not convinced of the overriding merits of the Anglo-Saxons, of the right of England to govern India, and of the infinite benefits India received from such government.

The political utterances of prominent leaders were likewise liberally adorned with hymns of praise to the virtues of the Anglo-Saxon race. Joseph Chamberlain said, "I believe that the British race is the greatest of governing races that the world has ever seen." Lord Cromer, the great British pro-consul in Egypt, believed that ". . . the Englishman, amidst many deviations from the path, will strive, perhaps to a greater extent than any other member of that [the European] family, to attain to a high degree of eminently Christian civilization. . . ." And Cecil Rhodes, who left much of his fortune to further the idea that the Teutonic peoples might rule the earth, said modestly, "We happen to be the best people in the world, with the highest ideals of decency and justice and liberty and peace, and the more of the world we inhabit, the better it is for humanity."[16]

But of course the exaltation of the virtues of the Anglo-Saxon by these Britons, and by many Americans of the same period also, carried with it the implicit and sometimes explicit derogation of other peoples. The conventional language of British officialdom referred to the non-European subjects of the Crown as "natives," whether of Africa, India, or Fiji, but the nonofficial language was more revealing of the true image of such people in the British mind.

In the Commons, Lord Stanley, scion of a noble British family prominent in political life, stated that the life of one British officer was, "measured by any rational standards of comparison, worth more than the merely animal existence of a whole African tribe." General Sir Garnet Wolseley, the outstanding British general of the colonial wars of the nineteenth century, referred to the West Africans as "so many monkeys." Lord Kimberley, a British Colonial Secretary, commenting on the possibility of the use of trial by jury in the West African colony of Sierra Leone, stated that, "A jury of Englishmen is a tolerable institution—a jury of Irishmen often intolerable—a jury of blacks I should say always intolerable."[17]

One result of the development of racist thought was that it tended to diminish the substantial degree of humanitarianism that had so profoundly influenced British policy in the earlier years of the century. With the "scientific" approach to race securing a hold on the minds of men, with doctrines of racial superiority increasingly one of the unspoken assumptions—and not always unspoken at that—affecting British policy, the earlier optimism about the educability of non-Europeans and the possibility of training them in the ways of constitutional practices known in British life diminished. Lord Macaulay had looked forward to the day when the public mind of India would be sufficiently expanded by contact with British law and education, and when good government would have trained Indians to the degree that they could undertake their own government. He also stated that when a time came when Britain could safely relinquish the power of government to Indians, "it will be the proudest day in English history." Sir Thomas Munro, one of the great administrators in British India in the first half of the nineteenth century, had stated that he could see no reason to doubt that if the British "pursue steadily the proper measures, we shall in time so far improve the character of our Indian subjects as to enable them to govern and protect themselves."[18]

But this early optimism diminished and was replaced by what one scholar called the "illusion of permanence" about British rule in India. There had never been complete agreement among Britons in their established preconceptions about India; not all would have looked forward, as did Macaulay and Munro, to the time of British withdrawal from India. But there seems to have been a distinct shift from the mixed optimism of the early years to the later pessimistic assumption that Indians, and other peoples as well, were condemned by their race to a condition of permanent inferiority and denial of participation in their own government, that the best they could hope for, and the best that Britain could give them was prolongation of the established forms of enlightened British paternalism. Britain would continue to carry the "white man's burden."

Philip Woodruff, a former officer of the Indian Civil Service, has summarized much of the relationship between English and Indian in the period about 1880 in his admirable study of the life of the British in India:

No one can deny . . . that there were things at this time of which an Englishman should feel ashamed and at which an Indian has a right to feel bitter. There was resentment because Indians were beginning to claim the equality the English had promised them. There was resentment because Indians were beginning to criticize the way the country was run. There were cases of rudeness to fellow passengers by train; there were cases—not many, but a sprinkling—of British soldiers injuring or even killing Indians when drunk and escaping with inadequate sentences. There was a feeling in the air summed up in a sentence overheard by Mrs. Moss King. At the outbreak of the second Afghan War, 'a young artillery officer put the present popular feeling in a nutshell. He said: "I know nothing of politics, but I do know that if a nigger cheeks us we must lick him." '

Racial arrogance there was then, and it was more widespread than at any time before or since. It was less necessary than it had been to meet Indians and to understand them, because there was more English society in India than ever before, because it was cheaper and quicker to go to England and because leave was taken more often. There was less isolation and there were more English women to talk to. 'Among women, who are more rapidly demoralised than men, abuse of "those horrid natives" is almost universal,' wrote Sir Henry Cotton. A process that had begun in the 'forties was accelerated; fewer and fewer Englishmen were identifying themselves thoroughly with the country. At the same time the English as a nation felt utterly secure, their preeminence in wealth and naval power unchallenged, their works manifestly approved by the Almighty.[19]

The British carried their beliefs of racial superiority into the administration of government. Despite such pledges as that given in 1833, when the Parliament renewed the charter of the East India Company, that "no subject of Her Majesty should, by reason of his religion, place of birth, descent, colour, or any of them be disabled from holding any place, office or employment under the Company," a pledge further renewed when the British government took over the administration of India in 1858, the administrative and military bureaucracy of nineteenth century India was almost exclusively British.

The theoretical legal equality of all subjects of the Crown formed but a thin and transparent disguise for the practical inequality that existed. There were Indians in the service of the Indian government, but only in subordinate positions. Entry into the Indian Civil Service, the central agency of administration in India, and the most powerful body of servants of the state, was effectively denied to Indians by a variety of circumstances. Some of these were admittedly of Indian creation. There were powerful influences in Hindu life against leaving India and travelling overseas. Those who did so were likely to find themselves ostracized when they returned to India. But it was British policy that decreed that entry exams for the Indian Civil Service had to be taken in London; thus the restrictions of the two societies, the Indian and the British, nicely combined to keep entry into the ICS narrowly in British hands.

There were other difficulties for the Indians. They had to match the British applicants in facility in the English language, and they had to meet the greater expenses of study in England and of travel there to take the examinations. Further, they had to take such exams when they were of the same age as English candidates, despite the fact that they generally needed more time for effective preparation. Efforts to get simultaneous exams in London and in India failed; nor did any greater success attend the efforts to get a flexibility in the age requirement that would have allowed Indians a better chance in the competitive struggle.

Despite all of these difficulties, some few Indians were successful in the competitive exams and received positions in the prestigious ICS. But when one of the first of these, Surendranath Banerji, was dismissed from that service because of his criticisms of the decisions of a British judicial officer, most educated Indians were persuaded that even the best that any Indian could bring in the way of education and intelligence was insufficient to break down the wall of exclusion the British had constructed around their administration of Indian affairs. As time went on, however, and the number of educated Indians increased, concessions were made, prompted not only by the agitation in India but by a liberalization of British attitudes. But as in so many other instances, the original impression that the British were concerned for the jealous preservation of their privileges endured long after the fact and continued to influence Anglo-Indian relations. Indeed, the concessions came so belatedly, and with such apparent reluctance, that the Indian impression of British hostility to the admission of Indians into the higher levels of administration was amply justified. Sir Bartle Frere, Governor of Bombay in the 1860's and one of the outstanding Anglo-Indian administrators of the period, described the British policy thus: "A rather pompous parade is made of a few crumbs of patronage which can now be thrown to Natives; and an opinion is implied, perhaps, rather than expressed, that this is quite as much as Natives or their advocates can expect. . . . I can imagine nothing more galling to a native possessed of any proper feeling than the self-satisfied, supercilious spirit which is occasionally apparent."[20]

The same pattern of discrimination against Indians prevailed in the military forces, both of the Company and later of the Crown. British policy denied to Indians in the military service any share in the command of troops or military administration, and after the Mutiny the more highly skilled specialist units, such as artillery and engineers, were confined largely to Britons. The most distinguished military historian of British India wrote of the career possibilities of the native Indian soldier under the company's regime,

It [military service] ceased to be a profession in which men of high position accustomed to command, might satisfy the aspirations, and expend the energies of their lives. All distinctions were effaced. The native service of the Company came down to the dead level of common soldiering, and rising from the ranks by a painfully slow process to merely nominal command. There was employment for the many; there was no longer a career for the few. Thenceforth, therefore, we dug out the materials of our army, from the lower strata of society, and the gentry of the land, seeking military service, carried their ambitions beyond the red-line of the British frontier, and offered their swords to the Princes of the native states.[21]

As with the Indian Civil Service, the British made concessions to the demands of Indians for wider opportunities in the military service and to the growing national consciousness among Indians. Up to the time of World War I, Indians with any command responsibilities had held their commissions from the Viceroy of India, a commission that was in all cases inferior to the Royal or King's commission. But in the pressures of war, Indians were increasingly associated with the officer corps of the army, and after the war, places were reserved in Sandhurst, the major English military training institution, for Indians; those who graduated received the Royal commission. By 1926 there were only forty-two Indian officers holding the Royal commission. But the rate of Indianization of the officer corps proceeded at a dignified pace between the wars, spurred somewhat by the creation of an Indian military academy; at the outbreak of war in 1939, there were some 600 Indian officers, and at the close of the war that number had jumped some twenty-fold. There were still very few Indians holding higher rank, however, despite the pressures of the war.

The racial animus implicit in this pattern of discrimination became all too glaringly apparent in the great disturbance in the European community during the 1880's over the so-called Ilbert Bill. This bill, sponsored by the Legal Member of the Viceroy's Executive Council, would have permitted Indian magistrates and justices to preside at the trials of Europeans. In a way, this was a return to the broad humanitarian values of men such as Lord Macaulay, for he had some fifty years earlier sponsored a comparable piece of legislation. But the

Ilbert Bill met with almost total resistance from Britons in India. Disregarding the fact that they were the principal beneficiaries of the structure of law and authority, and that their position in India was largely dependent upon the maintenance of the majesty of the British *raj*, they attacked that authority and did their best to humiliate it and force it to retreat in the face of lawlessness. Lord Ripon, the liberal Viceroy who favored the principle of the bill, was publicly insulted; entertainments at his residence were boycotted by nonofficial Europeans, and there was even a rather harebrained plan to kidnap the official representative of the Queen-Empress and ship him back to England as if he were some mutineer or pirate. The nature of the "debate," to dignify it beyond its deserts, is suggested by two contributions in the British-owned press in India, for day after day, infuriated Britons resorted to the columns of the press in the way in which, at home, they vented their spleen to the *Times*. "Britannicus" wrote to *The Englishman* of Calcutta that "The only people who have any right to India are the British; the so-called Indians have no right whatever." And the editor of the *Friend of India* editorially inquired, "Would you like to live in a country where at any moment your wife would be liable to be sentenced on a false charge, the Magistrate being a copper-coloured Pagan?" The whole effort humbled authority, for in the face of the agitation, and the fact that many in the Indian government also resisted the bill, it was withdrawn and an innocuous, face-saving compromise replaced it.

The agitation over the Ilbert Bill, and the revelation to an increasingly alert and discerning Indian public that the mighty British *raj* could be shaken by political uproar and protest, was a salutary lesson. Instructed, perhaps more implicitly than explicitly, by the British in the fact of their own inferiority in the arts of government, emotionally scarred by the lack of any real participation in the direction of their own society, Indians were likely to have continued to suffer from one of the most unfortunate aspects of colonialism: the sense of their own helplessness. What could they do against the remote and implacable power of the imperial structure? But the lesson of the Ilbert Bill's emasculation was clear. It made even more obvious the racial bias of the British community in India and their patent unwillingness to make any concessions to Indians; but it also made clear that organized political agitation could turn the government from an announced course of action.

The Ilbert Bill episode helped to end the frustration of the Western-educated Indians, familiar with the parliamentary history of the British people and the teachings of Burke and Bagehot, and to bring them in increasing numbers into the field of political activity. Fortunately there were exceptional Englishmen, precious leavens in the lump, who sympathized with Indian aspirations, and were willing to give what lead they could to Indian hopes for a wider share in their government.

One of them, Alan O. Hume, a former member of the Indian Civil Service, and son of the noted Radical of English political life, Joseph Hume, took a leading role in the founding in 1885 of the Indian National Congress, the great national organization that led in the long political agitation for Indian self-government. Sir William Wedderburn, another Briton who had been high in government councils, was a staunch advocate of Indian rights during the same period. A British business man, George Yule, was an early president of the Indian National Congress. Mrs. Annie Besant, the British leader of the theosophist movement, was one of the most active workers for Indian self-government in the first decades of the twentieth century. And in addition to these and others who might be named there were many in Britain who felt as so many had before them, that the proudest day that could come in Britain's relations with India would be the time when Britain could leave a strong and united India to be ruled by the Indian people themselves.

But there were many difficult confrontations to be experienced before that day came. And some of these revealed the abiding feelings of racial superiority and distrust felt by Britons toward their fellow subjects of the Crown, thus nullifying the good results that might otherwise have been expected from British political concessions to Indian demands.

The fact that the Indian Congress party existed, and that there was increasing demand among educated Indians for a larger place in Indian government, should not be construed as suggesting that India was a land of seething unrest. There remained in the Indian mind a substantial degree of faith in British good intentions for India; this is evident in the response that India and its people made to the crisis years of World War I. The British military forces in India were reduced to a virtual handful of men, and Indians of many creeds rallied to the Imperial cause for service both in military and civil life. A leading British statesman said that India had "bled herself white at the beginning of the war to supply the deficiencies of the Empire in troops, arms and guns."[22]

But if India contributed much, its people expected something in return. This sense of expectancy was heightened by the world-wide proclamations of Wilsonian doctrines of self-determination, and by the overthrow of other empires in Russia, Austria-Hungary, and Germany in the wake of the war. The British government was sensitive to these rising expectations in Indian life, and in August 1917 the Secretary of State for India made a historic pledge that the policy of the British government was to move as speedily as possible to the time when India would have self-government in the form that Canada and Australia had, and would be associated with such states as a self-governing member of the British Commonwealth of Nations.

The effects of this pronouncement were, however, gravely harmed by British repression of nationalistic outbreaks that occurred in postwar India. These outbursts grew from the accumulation of grievances gathered over the years, exacerbated by postwar unemployment, and by the proposed Rowlatt acts, one of which was designed to check the more anti-British Indian press. They were particularly serious in the area of northwestern India called the Punjab, and most serious of all in the city of Amritsar. There the riots led to the intervention of military forces, and in the efforts to disperse a crowd of some thousands milling about in a large enclosed square, the troops opened fire, and under the orders of their commanding officer, kept on firing for about ten minutes, until the crowd was dispersed, but with three hundred seventy-nine dead and over twelve hundred left wounded. This "Amritsar Massacre" shocked many in Britain, but in India it roused bitter anger and stimulated political agitation to altogether new levels of action. Contributing to this were arbitrary orders by other British officers after the Massacre, requiring all Indians riding in conveyances to alight when they met a British officer, and all who carried umbrellas against the Indian heat to lower them and come to a salute. Some Indians convicted of minor offenses were ordered to jump up and down and while doing so to compose impromptu verses in favor of martial law and British authority! The vaunted and usually genuine British concern for the due process of law went overboard in the anxiety and tension following the activities in the Punjab, and had they wished for it, those British responsible could not possibly have done more to promote further agitation and arouse Indian pride and nationalism. The Amritsar Massacre led the head of one of the most Anglicized of Indian families to turn his back on English ways, re-adopt much of the Indian manner of dressing and living, and plunge into Indian nationalistic activity. This man was Motilal Nehru, whose only son, Jawaharlal, was to become the first Prime Minister of an independent India. The Massacre also contributed greatly to the emergence of a man of genius, Mohandas Gandhi, as the leader of the Indian nationalist cause.

Gandhi was a revolutionary leader, but of a variety never seen before, in that the weapons he adopted were those of noncooperation and nonviolence. It is true that in the tension and pressures of the following decades, violence frequently boiled to the surface, and Gandhi himself was to fall to an assassin's bullet soon after the establishment of Indian independence. But without Gandhi's emphasis, the bloodshed might have been infinitely more than it was.

Of course, it has to be recognized that nonviolence was effective against the British where it might have failed against others. Bertrand Russell has remarked, and wisely, that nonviolence "depends upon the existence of certain virtues in those against whom it is employed." Few Britons would have felt that political power should grow out of the barrel of a gun. There was a great uproar in Britain over the Amritsar Massacre, for example, and widespread condemnation. Britons had little stomach for empire if it meant holding that empire only by force. As the Secretary of State for India rhetorically asked the House of Commons in London in the wake of the Amritsar disaster, "Are you going to keep your hold on India by terrorism and racial humiliation and frightfulness. . . ?" Most, though not all, would have answered for a strong rejection of any such possibility. The character of British political life and of British institutions banned any wholesale use of military force or of terrorism against Indian nationalism, even if such a course had any chance of success. In addition, the fact that Britain had just concluded a war which most Britons felt had been fought against Prussian terrorism in Europe reinforced this reluctance.

In such a situation the Gandhian tactic of nonviolence was of maximum effect. British authorities in India would arrest and imprison Gandhi and some of his followers on occasion, but the device seemed futile against those who seemed to court such punishment and went to prison rejoicing. So the British action in India was essentially a holding one, governed by recognition of the need for change, but also influenced by fear that change might be too hurried to be effective, that haste would create not simply waste, but chaos. Thus the British moved toward granting India self-government and then independence, jostled by the impatience of the Indians, by the weakening of the popularity of empire among their own people, and eventually, by the swift decline of British power in World War II. The Labor Government of postwar Britain announced almost peremptorily in 1946 that on August 15, 1947, Britain would abandon responsibility for the government of India and turn it over to whatever government in India could be formed to receive it.

The achievement of this independence brought India, and the other successor state to British India, Pakistan, into full legal equality with the other members of the British Commonwealth. Relations of India with these states—Canada, Australia, New Zealand, South Africa—had also for many years been impaired by racialism. The history of the relations of Indians with other communities of the British empire is a long and painful one. Paradoxically, India's relationship was best with those states, such as Australia, who would admit no Indians at all as permanent residents, so long as the restrictive legislation was not based on race, but on education or some other form of disqualification. The states that barred the migration of Indians were only exercising the form of sovereign authority that India hoped to have and use itself someday. Conversely, relations were worst with states that admitted Indians, but wanted them only as coolie labor and tried to hold them in second class status once admitted. South Africa was perhaps the most notorious offender in this, but she was not alone. In Kenya, Fiji, British Guiana, some of the islands of the British West Indies, Indians who had gone there frequently as contract laborers or under some form of indentured service found much hostility and little opportunity once their indenture was completed. India found itself and its people discriminated against both coming and going; policies of immigration restriction implied racial inferiority, and those of immigration encouragement, at least as carried out, meant the same thing. In these relations with the outside world, and especially with those that might be called sister states of the British empire, Indians suffered degradation and pain. This unhappy story continues today in the wake of the retreat of British power and the establishment of new independent nations from the former colonies; witness the flight of Indians from Kenya, the considerable racial antagonism between the native islanders and the Indians in Fiji, and the bitter political-cum-racial divisions existing in Guyana today. And perhaps the bitterest and unhappiest indication of all is the retraction of the British promise to Indians, given at the time of the granting of independence to Kenya, that if life in Kenya became too difficult, the Indians would be allowed entry to Britain. That promise has been shamefully nullified by an amendment that now allows only some thousand or more Kenya Indians into Britain each year. This may be an effective sop to prejudices of the British voters, but it is an unhappy revelation of the total collapse of even the minimal concept of a common citizenship under the Crown that prevailed in the hey-day of the Empire and *raj*.

The poet Claudian, who lived during the last years of the western Roman Empire, could write of the subjects of Rome, "We are all one people." For better or worse, this was never to be the story of the British empire; the forces of devolution, of nationalism, particularism, and disunity prevailed over the little there was of common subject-hood or status under the Crown. The development in the British empire was to a variety of nationalities, not to a single world-wide state. In this, there is much good, but the declining significance of the Commonwealth as a bridge between the old and new nations is a real loss. The arrogance of race was surely a major reason for this.

While the African experience as part of the British empire differed greatly from the Indian, one melancholy similarity was the existence of the same racial arrogance that had disfigured Anglo-Indian relations. One significant difference, however, lay in the African memories of the bloody and brutalizing slave trade. Westerners may plead in some small measure of extenuation that slavery and the slave trade was by no means confined to white exploitation of blacks; the slave trade was infinitely more common and widespread than that. Black enslaved black; the infamous trans-Atlantic traffic in slaves would not have been possible without the collaboration of blacks who captured blacks and of others who sold them into the hands of white slavers. Arabs were the principal slave traders in eastern Africa; and rather as a ironic comment, in the mid-nineteenth century there was a lively market in white Circassian females in Egypt, only one aspect of the operation of slavery in that land.

But with all this, the classic slave trade of the modern world was the shameful one which robbed Africa of its people and Africans of their lives and human dignity, and carried them across the Atlantic to give their life and labor for the enrichment of the white communities of the New World. India and the Indian people had no such horrifying experience in their relations with the West.

Africa prior to European conquest was a land of great cultural diversity, greater in some respects than that of India. Many Africans shared with much of India the faith of Islam. In the north, along the Mediterranean littoral, and in much of sub-Saharan Africa, the call of the faithful to prayer echoed daily, as it did for the hundreds of millions of the Islamic faith in Asia and the Middle East. As with India, Christianity had its island communities in Africa. The most notable citadel of Christian faith was Ethiopia, where the ancient Coptic version of the faith prevailed, but American and British humanitarianism had created small enclaves of Christianity in Sierra Leone and Liberia by the establishment of settlements for former slaves or those freed from the slaving vessels arrested in the illegal and notorious Middle Passage run across the Atlantic. And in Portuguese Africa, the rulers of those colonies had planted Catholic Christianity as they had in Goa and Dui on the Malabar coast of India. The greater part of tropical Africa, however, had little contact with such universal faiths; in those areas there was a variety of religious beliefs and practices, most of them reflecting the way the people lived and worked, providing sanction for their social laws and customs, and giving some measure of coherence to their societies. But if war is any test of the coherence, it is noteworthy that it was in the regions dominated by Islam and Christianity that European conquerors or would-be conquerors, such as the Italians in Ethiopia, encountered the greatest resistance.

There was a wide variation in the level of material culture among the African peoples. Africa in its past had produced many imposing political states, some of them rich and economically productive. Perhaps the greatest period of African history was during the centuries when many of the peoples south of the Sahara were most influenced by the Islamic civilization, then in its most flourishing condition. Ghana, Mali—not to be confused with the modern African states of the same names—Songhai, Kanem-Bornu were, among others, states of Africa that testify to the creativeness of the peoples of the sub-Saharan regions. The Islamic influence was even more apparent in the later trading city civilizations of East Africa.

All the way down the coastline of Somaliland, Kenya and Tanganyika, there sprouted urbanized Islamic communities, building in stone or coral rag, and wealthy enough, for example, to import such luxury goods as the stoneware of Siam and the porcelain of late Sung and early Ming China.[23]

At the opposite end of the scale were the peoples of the extremity of southern Africa, with whom Europeans came in contact in the long voyage around the Cape of Good Hope, and whom the Dutch got to know when the Dutch East India Company established its way station and refreshment center at the Cape in 1652. The Hottentots were a pastoral people, but beyond their flocks, they had little in the way of material wealth or culture, and the Bushmen of the Cape were even less developed materially, for they were still in the hunting stage of growth, not yet the pastoral folk their neighbors were. On a comparably poor level were the pygmy people of the Ituri forest area of the Congo basin.

Early European contacts with the people of sub-Saharan Africa widened the scope and the damage of the existing slave trade. African chiefs and merchants had engaged in the traffic before Europeans came along to increase the trade. Africans had been offered for sale in the markets of the Arab or Berber communities to the North, in the Middle East, and also in Europe itself. There were Africans in bondage even as far away as China. But it took the coming of Europeans and the opening of new markets for enforced labor in the New World to make the slave trade the central element it became in the economy of many African areas. For up to the time of the European contacts, the traffic in humans had been incidental to the sale of other commodities, such as ivory.

While there was a market and demand for slaves in Europe before the discovery of America, it was only with the opening of the opportunities of the New World that the trade began to develop into a major traffic and ultimately into big business. All of the maritime nations of Europe had a hand in this dolorous business; despite the pioneering efforts of Sir John Hawkins in the traffic in the sixteenth century, it was not until the latter part of the seventeenth century that Englishmen became deeply involved in the traffic. The Royal African Company was the chief English corporation in the trade, and it built up trading posts and fortifications on the west African coast, as well as trading connections with coastal peoples, in order to further the traffic. The eighteenth century was the hey-day of the slave trade and of the British participation in it. The immensity of the business may be appreciated from the fact that between 1783 and 1793, Liverpool ships—Liverpool was the center of British slaving activity—carried more than 300,000 slaves to America.

The prohibition of the slave trade by Britain and the United States in 1807 and 1808, later joined by other nations, and the long efforts at the strangulation of the illegal traffic, particularly by the British Royal Navy, compelled African trading communities to find new commodities for export. They had been tied in closely with the European trading interests and were too dependent on goods that Europeans alone could supply for them to be able to relinquish their European contacts; both they and the Europeans became interested in the development of "legitimate" trade as opposed to the now illegitimate slave trade. Since Britain took the leading role in the development of much of this trade, there grew up an "informal British empire" along much of the west African coast. This was motivated not only by trading interests, but also by humanitarian and missionary concern, as well as the British preoccupation for the suppression of the slave trade, a matter that naturally led them to an interest in those areas and people who continued in the traffic. In addition to these, there was a growing scientific and intellectual interest in the exploration of

Africa. A number of courageous explorers and travellers from many nations in Europe gradually lifted the ignorance and obscurity that made Africa the Dark Continent in the minds of Europeans.

None of this activity led to any push for European annexations in Africa; the value of the trade remained limited, and with the exceptions of such valuable seaports as Capetown, there was little strategic interest in Africa. If there was any major and overriding attitude that Britons had toward Africa, it was that Britain had a duty to extend the blessings of Christian civilization among the African people. A Parliamentary Committee summarized this attitude, with all its benevolence and essential arrogance, in 1837:

The British Empire has been signally blessed by Providence, and her eminence, her strength, her wealth, her prosperity, her intellectual, her moral and her religious advantages, are so many reasons for peculiar obedience to the laws of Him who guides the destiny of nations. These were given for some higher purpose than commercial prosperity and military renown. . . . Can we suppose otherwise than it is our office to carry civilization and humanity, peace and good government, and, above all the knowledge of the true God, to the uttermost ends of the earth?[24]

And the saintly Dr. Livingstone struck essentially the same note in a speech at Cambridge after one of his more strenuous exploratory efforts in Africa.

I know that in a few years I shall be cut off in that country which in now open; do not let it be shut again. I go back to Africa to try to make an open path for Christianity. Do you carry out the work which I have begun. I leave it to you.[25]

Undoubtedly Livingstone urged the "open path" chiefly for Christianity, but he also saw the possibilities of the growth of cotton in parts of Africa which were then very laboriously traversed; and this was a matter of some importance to an English cotton industry whose established supply was threatened by the imminence of civil strife in the United States.

While European penetration was opening up Africa, there was only slight interest in the formal annexation of territory on the part of any of the European states. The commercial or strategic advantages were too slight to lead to any such action. The only substantial British concerns were in the south, where the colonies of European settlement in the Cape and Natal, under British control, and those further in the interior controlled by the Boers, seemed to be involved in a endless series of frontier wars with natives and quarrels between Boer and Briton. It was not until the 1880's that the interests of European states reached beyond the coastal areas deep into the African interior, and extensive annexations followed.

The British occupation of Egypt in 1882, intended by the British government of the day to be only temporary, broke the general unwritten understanding that Africa was to be undisturbed, and opened up what has been called the "scramble for Africa." Within two decades following the English occupation of Egypt, European powers had engrossed practically all of Africa, with Britain acquiring the lion's share, something over three million square miles.

Since World War II, more than forty independent nations have emerged from the colonial territories appropriated by the European powers in this belated rush for annexation. For most of them, and thus for Africa as a whole, the period of European political domination was exceedingly brief, and yet one crammed full of change. Writing in 1967, a scholar in African history wrote:

There can be no escaping the fact that, for most of Africa, the events of the last fifty years before 1945 were more productive of profound revolutionary changes, and incomparably more decisive for future development, than any others since the coming of iron and the introduction of settled agriculture.[26]

The changes were revolutionary because few of the European administrators or rulers had any sense of an African culture worth respecting; in the story of British rule in Africa, there were no voices such as those of Sir William Jones, Warren Hastings, and others to urge consideration for the lore and learning, the culture of the native peoples, as there had been at one stage in India. Materially, African society seemed vastly more primitive than did Indian, hence less worthy of esteem. Also, although with some notable exceptions, Africans put up less resistance to European conquest than did Indians. Not that it was a series of bloodless military excursions; there was tribal and frontier warfare in many areas, but the apparently measureless strength of European states brushed much of this opposition aside with an almost careless ease. And Europeans, Britons no less than others, respected those who fought them effectively more than those who seemed incapable of waging any effective war. Kipling's tribute to the "fuzzy-wuzzy" of the Sudan as a "poor benighted heathen but a first-class fighting man" reflected a prevalent attitude. Further, by now there was nothing tentative about British Imperial authority. Backed with the experience of governing India, and armed with the triumphs of nineteenth century material, social, and intellectual advance, few Europeans doubted the ability of colonial control to improve vastly the condition of African life.

In actual administration, however, the British governed rather lightly and made little effort to transform the African into some form of black Briton. In part, this policy was based on the old desire for economy. Colonial communities were supposed to pay their own way in the world, with little if any direct subsidization, and since most of these communities were stark naked poor, the tasks of government were kept at the minimum level of peace keeping. One thing there was: an abundance of labor. Thus great efforts could be put into the construction of roads; these required little expensive capital equipment, and labor alone would suffice for the essentially primitive roads needed.

One of the notable forms of British authority was the pattern of "indirect rule" established by a great African pro-consul, Lord Lugard.[27] This simply sought to utilize the existing political leadership, emirs or chieftains, under the guidance of British residents. Thus a superstructure of British authority was created, but at a minimal cost of money and British administrators. In some respects, the system was akin to that prevailing in India for the native states, those areas still nominally ruled by native princes, but with British advisors and with defense and foreign relations in British hands. Indirect rule, however, was limited mostly to Nigeria.

One of the oddities of the British rule in Africa was the variety of legal forms it took. Britain never annexed Egypt; she simply controlled the land and administered its affairs without a legal termination of its sovereignty. The vast Sudan area to the south was administered as a condominium, nominally sharing authority with Egypt. Needless to say, the sharing was very one-sided. Personnel and policies were British; financial contributions, until a rather late date, were overwhelmingly Egyptian. In Sudanese affairs, Britain and Egypt had a joint bank account; but Egypt made all the deposits and the British wrote all the checks. Uganda was a protectorate, Tanganyika a mandated territory from the League of Nations after World War I. Nigeria, Sierra Leone, and Ghana were annexed colonial territories. The Rhodesias, north and south, started out as the granted lands of chartered companies. And after the South African War of 1899–1902, the four colonies of European settlement in southern Africa were quickly federated in the Union of South Africa, a self-governing dominion.

In all of these and other British territories, the European population was grossly outnumbered by the Africans. There were, of course, significant areas of European settlement. South Africa, the Rhodesias, and the highlands of Kenya attracted substantial numbers of European settlers. In these areas the white settlers took the best lands, and naturally controlled the productive capital, the political machinery, and the better-paying jobs. Many of the native peoples, deprived of their ancestral lands, were forced into labor on European-owned farms or mining ventures.

But European settlement was limited to areas that were regarded as healthy, and since the western areas had been notorious for centuries as a white man's grave, there were relatively few Europeans anxious to settle there; most of them were merchants and government officials. Despite the discovery of the efficacy of quinine for the control of malaria in the 1850's, and the recognition of the mosquito as the vector for the spread of yellow fever, the West African communities remained unattractive to white settlers, with the result that the bulk of land remained in African hands. British authority rebuffed efforts of some European interests to introduce plantation agriculture and thus preserved the African interest in their land. But despite such cushions against the impact of European ideas as indirect rule and land security, African culture reeled under the blow of Western authority and power.

Although some effective work in African languages and an occasional understanding and appreciative study of African culture had been done, there was little real knowledge of African life and society at the period when European powers were making their heaviest claims to African territory. In the European mind, Africans generally fell into the dismal category of "barbarians," tribal chieftains were "despotic tyrants," and the best thing that Europeans could do for Africans was to come to their rescue with the enlightened blessings of Western culture. Needless to say, such a simplistic view had much error, as well as some truth, and there was little in it to equip the Western officials or missionaries with an understanding of the native peoples. Indeed, in some mission circles it was believed so strongly that like appealed to like that it was felt that missionaries to such simple folk should be rather simple themselves, and not too well-educated or equipped with the knowledge of the ways of the world as to cost them the common touch.

The result was that even with the best of intentions, and not all Britons had these, clumsy hands were laid on African customs. The intricate tribal customs of marriage and morality, the sustaining sense of coherence and identity from kinship systems, the patterns of land ownership, the time-honoured rituals and ceremonies all felt the shock of Western criticisms and attacks. The complex community lives of numerous tribes came under grave tensions, if they were not shattered entirely, and left many an African psychologically disoriented. In addition, there were apparent contradictions in Christian teachings that Africans soon observed. Polygamous marriages fell sharply under the Christian ban, though Africans soon knew enough of the Old Testament to know that Abraham and many of his descendants had more than one wife. And there was the obvious contradiction between the ethics of Christianity and the practice of Christians.

The displacements and disruptions of African life would have been a substantial price, at best, to pay for the admitted progress in many areas that Europeans brought with them. But the price was even greater when it was accompanied, as it all too frequently was, by the loss of lands, and the enforced creation of a landless proletariat that was turned into a pool of cheap labor for Europeans. Accompanying this was the dreary litany—so frequently heard in regions of the United States—of the white man's mythology of the black, encapsulated in the dictum, "They're just like children." But they never suggested that their own children might be like the blacks. There were numerous other ways in which the whites created and perpetuated the traditional views of the African, all of them reflecting the sense of racial superiority.

All of this tended to create the situation where the white man, whatever his worth, was always something, or somebody, simply by virtue of his whiteness—and the black less than human, simply by the curse of being one of the descendants of Ham or on some other irrational basis. White settlers' communities thus tended to become little pink or white islands of smugness in the sea of color surrounding them, holding the power, position, possessions, and pride denied to the other race.

There is, of course, another side of the story. Jomo Kenyatta, the first president of independent Kenya and long a leader in the struggles for the independence of that African area, acknowledges the introduction of "progressive ideas" by the Europeans into African life:

They include the ideas of material prosperity, of medicine and hygiene and literacy which enable people to take part in world culture.[28]

Yet even in some of these benefits there was a real danger that a people concerned for the preservation of its culture might deplore. Too often the introduction of literacy ended the oral traditions that had enriched the life of a society through the generations and substituted an imperfect command of another tongue. Not in every sense is the substitution of Western knowledge for Eastern or African custom a total gain.

But it should also be recalled, in this day when the offense of colonialism or imperialism is so high on the calendar of crimes, that this is not something that can be imputed to the whites alone. Black Power is oppressing the black masses in Haiti, for instance; blacks war against blacks in the bitter fratricide of Nigeria; and the blacks of Africa cooperated with the whites in the creation of the slave trade. All men, white, black, yellow, and red are quite equally capable of oppressive abuse of power, and there seems to be no peaceful deterrent to this evil that men do each other.

The

Decline

of Power

Great Britain has lost an empire and has
not yet found a role.

DEAN ACHESON

Easter Monday was observed in Dublin, Ireland in 1916 in a manner
unusual in Catholic lands. Of course, the times themselves were unusual. The great powers of Europe were spilling the blood of their
sons in frightful and costly combat, and thousands of Irishmen had
volunteered for service in the British army and were adding laurels to
the fame of their forebears who had served in those ranks in preceding
generations. But in Dublin there hung a banner that flaunted its indifference to the great European conflict and spoke only of Irish
freedom. Across the front of Liberty Hall, a center of trade union
activity in Dublin, the banner proclaimed "We fight not for King or
Kaiser, but for Ireland." In keeping with that militant note, in Dublin

and throughout the land small bands of Irishmen had formed para-military units in apparent preparation for the time when they might be able to strike the needed blow for Irish freedom.

The British authorities in Ireland, and most Irishmen themselves, had regarded such activity with a certain amount of tolerance. Govern-ing officials in Dublin Castle felt that it was perhaps better to let the lads play at soldiering and thus work off steam, than to stir up a storm by trying to suppress them. But there were aspects of the situation that made continuation of this tolerant policy impractical, and one of these was the chance that the Germans might seek to bring arms to the Irish "rebels" and open up a second front in the British Isles them-selves. The possibilities in this had certainly not escaped the Irish leadership, and they had formed rather clumsy plans for the landing of a cargo of German arms in western Ireland to coincide with an armed uprising in the capital city and throughout Ireland. The vigi-lance of British naval forces prevented the landing of the promised German arms, and division within the ranks of the rebels prevented the uprising from occurring as planned. But for many of the national-ist units in Dublin, regardless of the confusion, the hour of Irish free-dom had come. Britain's difficulty was Ireland's opportunity, and Britain would probably never again be in as desperate a situation as when locked in mortal conflict in France. And so on Easter Monday morning the rebels marched to seize what they regarded as the strategic centers of Dublin. In so doing they set off a blaze in Ireland that ended with the burning of British power from much of the land.

Rebel bands began the uprising by taking several important loca-tions within the city and setting up road blocks and strong points to check the movement of British troops. As the centerpiece of their activity, a group of rebels seized the main post office of Dublin on Sackville Street. Later, under the portico of this building, one of their leaders read an Irish Declaration of Independence to a small crowd of onlookers and curiosity seekers, most of whom either seemed indiffer-ent to or actually tittered over the sonorous phrases.

For almost a week, street battles raged in Dublin as the British mobilized their forces to regain command of the rebel-held points. The rest of the country did not rise in support of the rebels, and at the end of the week they were compelled to yield. Court-martialed for armed rebellion against the Crown in time of war, some sixteen of the leaders were later executed by firing squad. (Among those spared was Eamon De Valera.) But by the manner in which they tried and executed them, the British helped these men to win a triumphant martyrdom. The delay in carrying out the death sentences, and the fact that some of the rebels had to be patched up from their wounds in order to be shot, gained for them a sympathy and admiration that their military folly had denied them. Ireland's great poet, W. B. Yeats, intoning the names of some of the fallen leaders, wrote

> We know their dream; enough
> To know they dreamed and are dead;
> And what if excess of love
> Bewildered them till they died?
> I write it out in a verse—
> MacDonagh and MacBride
> And Connolly and Pearse
> Now and in time to be,
> Wherever green is worn,
> Are changed, changed utterly:
> A terrible beauty is born.[1]

Not for the first, nor perhaps the last time in history, the final word was with the poet. For the dream of Irish freedom, and the manner of death of the men who had sought martyrdom for it, took hold of the minds and hearts of an increasing number of Irishmen. Spurred by memories of historic wrongs between British and Irish, and by the doctrines of self-determination then being proclaimed to the postwar world by the oracular American president, more and more Irishmen took arms in a guerrilla war against the British in the months after the Armistice. The struggle was bloody and bitter—the most bitter of all the challenges to British power during the decline of the British empire. Terror was used on both sides, and on a scale larger than ever before. Indeed, in the guerrilla tactics and the terrorism, the Irish struggle for independence was an unhappy portent of the political world yet to come. At last, sickened by the brutality of the struggle and weary to death of war, the British negotiated with some of the Irish leaders a treaty that established an Irish Free State, and accorded it the same power of self-government as that of Canada and other dominions of the British Crown.

With the exception of the Easter Rebellion and the subsequent fighting in Ireland, however, the bloody years of World War I brought remarkable testimony of the loyalty of the peoples of the empire. There were some troubles in Africa; in 1914 an old, unreconciled Boer led a small uprising that was speedily crushed by a government led by his former comrades-in-arms in the South African war. And in Central Africa, one of the early leaders of black nationalism led an even more feeble and abortive uprising against what he regarded as conscription of Africans for service in the British forces. But elsewhere throughout the lands of the British Crown, the response to Germany's challenge to the existing order of world power was all that the most ardent British imperialist might desire, and far exceeded the anticipations of nineteenth century partisans of empire. One of these had once written of the folly of the expectation that Canadians and Australians would ever come to Britain's aid in a struggle over such lands as Serbia or Luxembourg.[2] But they came in hundreds of thousands, adding to the British army the weight of their manpower and a fighting punch that exceeded their numbers. India and the other subject areas of the empire responded in a manner comparable to that of the self-governing states. Relying on Indian loyalty, British forces in India were stripped to the smallest size, and hundreds of thousands of Indians entered the ranks of the army for service on the fighting fronts in Asia and Europe. The war amply revealed the power of the ideal of Imperial loyalty to energize and mobilize the resources of a vast empire.

At the close of the war, Britain seemed to emerge even more engorged with territories and charged with Imperial responsibilities. True enough, this was supposed to be a peace without conquest and annexations, but there were many cynics and scoffers who saw in the system of mandates under the League of Nations nothing more than a polite disguise for old fashioned conquest, and of such mandates, Britain received the greatest share, especially in Africa and the Middle East. After the parcelling out of the new mandates, it was even more difficult for the sun to set on the British empire.

Yet behind this façade of greater Imperial power and authority there were signs and portents of declining power. Basic was the fact that the existing world order, which Britain had sacrificed so much to defend, was shattered, perhaps beyond repair. The nineteenth century fabric of trade and finance, the delicate web of international economic relationships which had been built up under British leadership during the previous hundred years, seemed to have suffered irreparable damage. The physical devastations of war were quickly remedied; but the statesmen of Europe and America spent years wrestling with the problems of reparations and war debts in an effort to recreate something of the same type of functioning world economic order that Britain had rather unconsciously designed in the nineteenth century. The measure of their failure is indicated by the onset of the great depression of the 1930's. Of course, this was due not only to the disruption of the patterns of world trade and finance, but to numerous flaws existing in the domestic economies of many of the European nations and also the United States. But again, Britain as the leading trading nation of the world was certainly among the more adversely affected.

Under the impact of the war and the depression, Britain gradually abandoned the free-trade policy that had been central in her relations with the rest of the world for about a century. In its stead came a host of regulations, quotas on imports, and various other protective devices. The state that had once boldly placed its faith in its capacity to compete with all comers in the markets of the world was now concerned to preserve even its limited domestic market for itself. Behind this change there was, of course, more than just the effects of war and depression, disastrous as those had been.

Accompanying this decline in trade and industry was the weariness arising from the costliness of the war both in life and wealth, and with this weariness a serious questioning of the vaunted superiority of Western civilization. Belief in this superiority had furnished the moral basis for imperialism. But after the horrors of the recent slaughter, where were those values now? Could a people or civilization that had brutalized itself in so terrifying a manner presume to instruct the rest of the world in morality or ethics? There were many who doubted.

Then there was the large-scale attack on empire and its works coming from the Marxists, now reinforced by their conquest of one of the great states of the European order, Russia, and by their power in other lands through the existence of large Communist and Socialist parties. Despite the substantial differences between Socialist and Communist groups, both tended to read the record of Imperial activities from the same scroll. Imperialism to them was a direct result of the inadequacies and injustices of the capitalist order at home; its chief purpose was the economic exploitation of native peoples.

The decline in the hold of empire on the minds of the British people was reflected in their acceptance of the recognition of Irish independence, and in their willingness to see the constitutional structure of the empire changed. Of course the record of constitutional arrangements within the empire had been one of constant devolution, as frequently suggested before, but this devolution now reached its logical conclusion in the transformation of empire into Commonwealth. An Imperial Government that had already given the powers of internal self-government to the white dominions recognized the growing maturity of these states by accepting their right of withdrawal from the empire and by acquiescing in their right to control their own foreign affairs. Much of this came without explicit statement, but was implicit in the famous Statute of Westminster of 1931 which acknowledged that the senior states of the Commonwealth were legally equal to the United Kingdom.

But such devolution was altogether natural in the light of the history of the empire. More controversial was the problem of the status of India, and involved in the fate of India, the government of the other non-European states of the empire. Under the pressure of the war, and in response both to emergent Indian nationalism and the widespread Indian support during the conflict, the British government had issued the famous Montagu Pledge in 1917, promising speedy extension of self-government to India, with the eventual attainment of responsible government, and the inclusion of India in the ranks of the self-governing dominions. Each step along this path was accompanied by greater Indian impatience for more rapid progress, and by cries among some British politicians and critics that the pace of events was already too great for India's good, and that the "fairest jewel in the imperial crown" was being incontinently thrown aside at the behest of radical politicians and an Indian fakir called Gandhi. Amid the agitation and the occasional riots that swept through major Indian cities, and the campaigns of civil disobedience that Gandhi was able to evoke among the people, progress in constitutional change was relatively rapid, and India stood on the edge of self-government when Hitler plunged Europe into war once again in 1939.

As with Ireland in World War I, Britain's difficulty in the second war seemed to create India's opportunity. But the Indian response to the situation was mixed. There were a few who joined the ranks of Britain's foes and formed an Indian unit that fought by the side of the Japanese after that nation joined the combat; and on the other side of the ledger, valiant divisions of the Indian army fought in Africa and Europe once again side by side with the British and other Imperial forces.

The dilemma of the Indian political leaders was great: how to serve the cause of Indian independence without aiding the Nazi and Japanese cause. Their plea was essentially that India free would more gladly and effectively contribute to the allied cause than India bound; the British response was that the transfer of power would best await the end of the war, for any such transfer during war would simply add confusion to the complexities of war, and damage the general cause of freedom. In the end the British time table prevailed; it was not until after the war that India received from the hands of a Socialist Labor government in Britain the independence so long sought by most of its political leaders.

In the acceptance of independence for India, Pakistan, and also

Ceylon, the British had acknowledged in fact what they had so long conceded in theory, the legitimacy of the aspiration of Asian peoples for self-government. The translation of theory into fact was hastened by the manifest postwar weakness of Great Britain, by the preoccupation of the British people with their own domestic concerns, and by their subsequent unwillingness to bear the burdens of empire any longer. To have continued to hold a rebellious India in political subordination would have been a grievous burden indeed. But with the granting of Indian independence Britain lost command of much of the strength that had been the basis of British power east of Suez. The empire that had been built up during the nineteenth century in Burma and Malaya was irretrievably weakened by the loss of control over India's manpower and resources. The recognition of Burmese independence, and British efforts to create a viable Malaysian state as a successor to British power in the Malay states, followed rapidly on the heels of the withdrawal from India, and to a great measure was ended with the stated British decision to abandon the Singapore base in the early 1970's. Though the military value of Singapore might appear questionable in the light of the ease of its conquest by the Japanese in 1942, it had been useful for the deployment of British power during the suppression of the Communist uprising and guerrilla war in Malaya. It was also useful later in the confrontation with Indonesia when that nation's leader, Sukarno, attempted to conquer Malaysia by tactics of infiltration and internal subversion. Regardless of the bitter memories of Japanese victories in the early months of the war in the Pacific, Singapore still stood in the mind of many as the strongest token of the British presence in the East, and the decision to withdraw from it came as a distinct shock not only to the new states of Malaysia and Singapore, but even to the more substantial communities of Australia and New Zealand. Yet, just as in the period of power the tide of empire had seemed to sweep inexorably forward, carrying British authority across the distant seas and into many remote corners of the globe, the ebbing tide now drew back just as inexorably. The demolition of empire went forward with dramatic speed, and the names of new nations appeared on the maps of the world in place of the former imperial red of British authority. Of course, Britain was not alone in the de-colonization process; other former imperial states such as France and Holland also relinquished control of their domains.

In the near aftermath of the age of European hegemony, it is perhaps an impossible and profitless task to try to assess the varying legacies left by imperial power in the countries it controlled, and in the minds of the people it ruled. The air is still full of discordant cries, many of them emanating from Communist states whose lust for power is no less than that of any of the imperial powers of the eighteenth and nineteenth centuries. A roundhouse denunciation of colonialism or imperialism is good for a solid round of applause any day at the United Nations Assembly meetings, and indeed, seems at times to be the staple item of such meetings. In the midst of the continuous hurling of abuse at former colonial powers it is difficult for any calm assessment to be made, yet certain conclusions may be drawn even at this early date.

Any evaluation, even the most casual, of the age of European power and the British part in it, must start with a recognition of the fact that the forces that created the vast imperial domains of Britain and other states were those that also created the modern world order. The increasing capacity for political organization, the control over the arts of production, the greater mobility of men and goods, the scientific advances of man, endowing him with power both over nature and over the rest of mankind not similarly blessed—these forces created the modern world and the imperial states along with it.

A leading Swiss observer has remarked that the colonization of the world by Europe was neither a chain of crimes nor a chain of beneficence; it was the birth of the modern world. Perhaps that statement might be modified: the age of European hegemony was the *result* of the birth of the modern world in Europe; the imperialism of the European powers was the extension of that modern world throughout the globe. And one fact is apparent, that none of the people or states pulled into the modern world by the intervention of European power is at all anxious to turn back the clock and revert to its precolonial condition, even if it were at all possible. Indeed, nearly all of the governments of former colonial territories are consumed by a passion to industrialize their lands in as Western a fashion as possible. This passion has led some of them into extravagant economic programs far beyond the capacity of their peoples to sustain, with subsequent economic disaster; the records of Ghana and Indonesia are perhaps the most obvious cases. The same Swiss commentator called this spread of industrialization colonialism's historic justification, but no such sweeping verdict is altogether acceptable. For some non-European states have achieved modernity without experiencing colonial thralldom; Japan is the most notable. Thailand too preserved its nominal independence during the period of European imperialism, and one would be loath to conclude that it is not as much part of the modern world as its neighbor Burma, which was formerly under British rule. On the other side of the picture, certainly most of the former colonial territories of Africa are closer to membership in the modern world than Ethiopia, the solitary African state that escaped colonial control, save for the brief period of Italian rule that ended with World War II. Thus for the question of whether colonial states were assisted to modernity by Western rule there is not a simple answer. Some undoubtedly were, and might never have attained the degree that they currently have without Western prodding; one or two others got there unassisted, though not without the urgent awareness that if they did not stir themselves, they were likely to fall under Western control.

The loss of strength in the European nations through the attrition of the two world wars (an Indian historian has called these the "civil wars" of Europe) was accompanied by the rise of nationalism, the great modern secular religion, in colonial territories. This was a most natural development. Britons who could sing in their churches the words of Cecil Spring Rice's hymn,

> I vow to thee, my country, all earthly things above,
> Entire and whole and perfect, the service of my love

were hardly in a position to wonder about the spread of nationalist ideas among the peoples they governed. Similar sentiments appeared among the subject folk; like ruler, like ruled.

Indeed, the emergence of some form of nationalism was almost a social necessity. The Western impact had fragmented and destroyed old groups and associations among non-Western peoples; tribal loyalties frequently disintegrated as the colonial rule opened up new opportunities and closed down old ones in tribal societies. The misfit or the rebel now no longer had to defer to traditional tribal authority, but could escape to the new towns founded by trade and commerce. Tribal warriors, deprived of their function by the peace established by colonial authority, sought employment in the mines opening up, on the construction crews for roads and railroads, or on the docks of the shipping centers. The stability created by colonial power meant that one could travel from the tribal lands with security; thus the drift away from the traditional territory, with its controls and taboos, got under way.

At the same time a new élite was emerging, one that had some training in the culture of the ruling state. There was a need for this, since the business of the ruling state could not be carried on without some degree of collaboration from the native peoples. And this was not the only reason for the growth of this élite; much of it resulted from the labor of missionary groups who had established schools and training centers among Asians or Africans. The consequences of this sort of education were apparent to the discerning even before the outbreak of World War I. Sir Harry Johnston, an outstanding British administrator in Africa, wrote in 1912:

The idea that there would ever be any serious demand on the part of the colonial peoples for a voice in their own taxation and government . . . scarcely disturbed any average imperialist. . . . But unfortunately for the ideals of the imperialist Britain of twenty years ago, education was permeating the British Empire in all directions . . . . Missionary societies were everywhere founding schools, colleges and universities, attempting to make black, brown and yellow people think and act like white Christians. . . . impressing them over and over again that once they were Christian and civilized, or even civilized without being Christian, they were the equal of any man, no matter of what colour or race.[3]

This concern, even passion for education as one authority has called it, led to the production of a class of Western-educated men who frequently found there was no real opportunity to use the learning or skills they had acquired, and who also found, far too frequently, that their laboriously acquired education did not open the doors to either the authority or the social life dominated by their European rulers. That this new Western-trained élite should seek first to join their rulers, and then being rebuffed, to supplant them, was surely a natural course. They found among the displaced rural workers and former tribesmen the raw material for a political following; they found in the idea of nationhood an organizing principle and institution to replace the older tribal forms that had been shattered. Of course, the hold of the older loyalties was more tenacious than many had expected, and the demands of the new nationalism heavier, so that some of the new nations of Africa, such as Nigeria, have been wracked by civil strife rooted in, among other things, ancient tribal hatreds. But it should be recalled that the nation-state was a long time aborning in European life, and that its sudden emergence among Asian or African peoples is no more to be expected than instant tolerance in Western lands.

What was the British legacy to the peoples they once ruled and to whom, in the last decade or two, they have granted independence? There are a variety of ways of appraising this legacy. It may be measured against an impossible ideal, and against that it is sadly wanting, but then so are all other human accomplishments. Or it may be measured against the legacies that other colonizing states left to their colonial peoples, and against this it is at least satisfactory, if not praiseworthy. One notable fact is that although at first the British rarely granted independence to a major colony except under some duress, it was equally rare for such duress to reach the level of major conflict, Ireland being the notable exception. Of course, there has been more than occasional conflict, but the conflict has, as likely as not, been between contenders for the right to succeed to the power the British were about to relinquish, rather than directly with the British to force them out.

The two forms of confrontation frequently became involved one with the other, each contending party blaming and attacking the British for not bequeathing their power to it. But even with this sort of conflict, and with other and more direct anti-British activity, the dismantling of empire went forward under conditions of general peace, and frequently of some good will. The British empire, as we have seen, was never a military state in its government, and the manner of its demolition again attests to this. In all, it strongly indicates that one of the major elements of the British inheritance to former colonial peoples was the idea that civil authority is superior to military, and that the military officer must be the servant and not the master of the state. This principle has not always been adhered to; there are military men who hold power in areas formerly under British rule. But this seems to be due more to the paucity of effective political leadership and to the fact that trained officers are frequently members of the better educated groups in the society. It does not necessarily indicate an abandonment of this tradition, though perhaps it is yet too early to draw a final conclusion.

All the British colonies were regarded by their colonial rulers, sooner or later, as prospectively self-governing states. The illusion of permanence of British authority, strong in the nineteenth century, could not survive the colossal shocks of historic change and of the great European wars of this century, nor could the colonial rulers or even the most benighted and stone age colonial areas ignore the fact that many colonies had been granted self-government. So the governing philosophy for the colonial empire was not that of assimilation to British power and to British life, but rather that of encouraging the planting and cultivation of institutions of government that might eventually—and here was frequently the rub—flower into self-government and independence. The process goes forward even today. In one of the most unpromising areas of the world, New Guinea, the Commonwealth of Australia is laboriously engaged in an effort to bring the people of the more than seven hundred tribes of the eastern portion of the island to an effective participation in the institutions of parliamentary government. In this effort, the Australians are following substantially in the British tradition.

In their acceptance of the fact that they would ultimately withdraw from power in the various colonies, even if at no foreseeable date, and also in their pattern of indirect rule, that is, of governing through the established institutions of the governed as much as possible, the British were recognizing, perhaps unconsciously, the right of the governed to their own cultural identity. Of course, the weight of an aggressive culture lay behind British rule, and standards of British morality demanded abolition of "abhorrent" native practices, but with it all there was at least a modicum of regard for native ways and culture. The British never consistently sought to turn colonial people into black or brown Britons. The French followed the other course, and tried to turn their subjects into Parisians. One result has been that since independence, the assertion of cultural identity among Africans has been stronger in the former French ruled areas than those of the British.

In these respects then, the British policy looked forward to a time when the people they ruled would take their place among the self-governing of the world. In many cases, however, they acted as if they had an infinity of time in which to attain this objective and an equally infinite degree of native patience. But they were surprised by time and overtaken by history. The illusion of permanence was shattered by events in Europe and by the increasing demands of subject peoples for control of their own affairs. Of course, there was British reluctance to accept the new situation; it was a bitter medicine for many to take. But the costliness of conflict in days of straitened British finances, and the futility of a series of little wars for the maintenance of a colonial authority that was increasingly at odds with the spirit of the time and the widely held faith in the right of self-government, became quickly apparent to the pragmatic British. In the end, the British were almost jostling some colonial peoples to self-government in an unseemly haste to free themselves of colonial responsibilities. But in an imperfect world, there is little time for perfect solutions to human problems; the choice had been made in the judgment of mankind, outside the Communist world at least, that any kind of self-government is better than colonial good government. Counsels of patience and perfection were unacceptable to those seeking their "freedom." The British worked to prevent disaster when the day for their withdrawal came, by speeding up their efforts to equip the colonial peoples with the instruments of a modern society. This accounted in part for the sudden proliferation of agencies of the Colonial Office that operated in colonial areas, for the passage of the Colonial Welfare and Development Act, and for the substantial sums that Britain poured into her colonial territories on the eve of her relinquishment of control over them and also after severance of the colonial connection. In part this was an admission of past indifference, but in part also a recognition of her responsibility to launch any new state upon the troubled sea of independence with as seaworthy a vessel as possible. Not all of these craft have had happy voyages, but to date, none of them has sunk.

Nearly all, if not all of them, entered upon their independence with ideas and institutions largely drawn to British design, and with part of their administrative personnel British and the rest trained in British methods, even though for some the training was somewhat meagre. In general, Britain gave the leadership of the new states the best she had in skill and education. Many of them were graduates of the most distinguished British universities; others were graduates of the numerous new universities that appeared in the colonial world in the post-World War II period. These new universities sought immediate academic acceptance by having their students submit to examinations prescribed by British schools, such as the University of London. This meant high academic standards, but often at the price of creating too élitist a concept of education, and also of establishing institutions of higher learning perhaps not sufficiently attuned to local needs. The work of education, both for graduates of institutions of higher learning and for the masses of population of the new states, was far from complete. One can lament, with one notable authority on African history, that there were not another fifty years in which the new states could be trained for independence. Yet the whole process of dismantling the empire—even though it was carried forward in haste, and at the end with the British as impatient to rid themselves of the colonial burdens as colonial peoples were to take independence—was carried out with good British intent, and with no evidence of malicious satisfaction at the mess that would prevail when they departed, though some might reasonably say *Après nous, le déluge.*

The ideas and institutions bequeathed to the new states were the tried and tested institutions of government and law that had matured in the British Isles: parliamentary government, the maintenance of the rights of the individual through adherence to the due process of law, the operation of courts free from political control or influence, freedom of speech, press, and assembly, the supremacy of civil authority over the military, the later development of the sense of the responsibility of the state for the maintenance of a minimum standard of welfare for its citizens. Of course, these admirable concepts have not been universally honored. Parliamentary government disappeared in Ghana with the rise of personal dictatorship, and that in turn gave way to military rule; Nigeria, the largest of the British areas of West Africa to receive independence, and the state from which most was expected, dissolved in a bitter civil-tribal warfare. In East African states such as Tanzania, one-party rule supplanted limited parliamentary government. And on a greater scale, parliamentary government in Pakistan seemed incapable of effective rule and was supplanted by presidential rule by former military leaders.

For the British were apt to be content with the creation of the forms of government as known at Westminster, without concern about the assumptions and values which alone make the Westminster form possible. In at least one notable case, Uganda, the parliamentary form of government existed before there was sufficient political interest among the people to create and sustain political parties. (A prominent member of the first independent Ugandan government admitted that Britain had handed his state its independence on a platter.) And a more general indictment would surely be that the British imparted and their former subjects learned the art of government without learning the art of legal opposition to government.

But even with this spotty record, the ideal of representative government in some form remains, and may even return, though with modifications necessary for local conditions, in several of the states in which it has for the moment disappeared. It is, after all, not necessarily of universal validity; the newly independent peoples must, as much as the world allows them, work out their own political forms in the long run, but these forms will certainly have a considerable measure of the British inheritance in them.

In their external relations, most of the newly independent lands have retained membership in the British Commonwealth; their political leaders foregather periodically with those of the United Kingdom and other states of the Commonwealth in London for the discussion of general problems. The two notable exceptions are South Africa and Burma. The former withdrew from the Commonwealth under pressure of condemnation of its racial *apartheid* policy in the early 1960's, and Burma chose not to join the Commonwealth when she attained her independence in 1947.

Of course, there is vastly less solidarity in Commonwealth relationships than there was a decade or so ago when the only members were the United Kingdom, the white dominions, and by sufferance, India. Community of interest has diminished with the inclusion of

African and Asian member states. The problems of Africa have only peripheral interest to Australia or Canada; the Southeast Asian and Pacific concerns of Australia and New Zealand are not shared by most of the other Commonwealth lands, and only marginally by the United Kingdom. Increasingly there seems justice in the judgment by one prominent British political figure that the Commonwealth is a "transparent fiction." But such fictions may still have a purpose. Periodic consultation, and the broader perspective that sometimes comes from it, is yet of value; the wider familiarity with the problems of other lands can be of much use. It is too early to dismiss the Commonwealth relationship as of no value; it may slowly decline into innocuous desuetude, or it yet may evolve under the pressure of circumstances, perhaps with regional associations, into some means of bringing the varying skills that have developed in many lands of the Commonwealth to the aid of those without such skills.

Some years ago a former American Secretary of State, Dean Acheson, rather raised the hackles of some Britons by saying that in the last few decades Britain had lost an empire and had not yet found a role to play in the world without it. Despite some British annoyance, it seems a just appraisal. Of course, it must be said that the United Kingdom has relinquished her power and authority gracefully and with dignity. Members of the royal family have gone gravely abroad to preside at ceremonies involving the lowering of the British flag and the hoisting of one of the many new flags that have taken its place. Strange new names have replaced the names of the colonial areas, and strange faces and costumes appear when leaders of the new states attend gatherings in London or come to confer with their former rulers. Much of the shock of the loss of command has been concealed behind the facade of the cooperative Commonwealth. But the diminished power of Britain has on occasion been too apparent to be disguised. The Suez Canal debacle of 1956 revealed the impotence of Britain in an area where once her writ was virtually law. The studied defiance of British orders, objections, and reprisals by a white Rhodesia that seems intent on joining South Africa in *apartheid,* and the inability of Britain to mitigate the Nigerian civil war have revealed clearly the decline of British power in areas of its former authority. From this there is naturally a certain trauma; even the British cannot accept it all with total equanimity of spirit, and irritation sometimes flares out in attacks on those, such as the United States, who have succeeded them in the seats of world authority. But this is minimal considering the fearful rapidity of the British decline in power, and also the fact that much of this power was lost in the hard years of war against Hitler's Germany. The Britons, in their economic distress, must have found the prosperity of postwar Germany galling.

Practically, the question of the British place in the world of the later twentieth century remains unanswered. Reluctantly, the British have accepted that they are part of Europe, but the recollections and ties of Imperial connections and Commonwealth associations are still strong, and for many British families are likely to remain so as some of their members continue to migrate to Canada, Australia, and New Zealand. Britons, especially of the older generation, can be forgiven for looking back nostalgically to the days of Imperial grandeur. And even for those who cannot share these memories there is gratification in the fact that under the aegis of its power and with the guiding influence of its example, Britain has called into existence some thirty of the present nations of the world. Surely this is no small achievement.

Notes

Chapter 1

1. Carlo M. Cipolla, *Guns, Sails and Empires: Technological Innovation and the Early Phases of European Expansion, 1400–1700* (New York, 1965), p. 137.

2. Donald F. Lach, *Asia in the Making of Europe* (Chicago, 1965), Vol. I, Book Two, 834.

3. Cipolla, *op. cit.*, p. 137.

4. *Ibid.*, pp. 80–81.

5. Elaine Sanceau, *Indies Adventure* (London, 1936), p. 47.

6. Albuquerque, Alfonso de, *Commentaries* (Hakluyt Society Publications, Old Series, No. 53), p. 117.

7. *Ibid.*, No. 62, p. 259.

8. *Ibid.*, No. 62, p. 262.

9. Lawrence Stone, "Elizabethan Overseas Trade," *Economic History Review*, 2d ser., II, No. 1, 51.

10. Ralph Davis, *The Rise of the English Shipping Industry in the Seventeenth and Eighteenth Centuries* (London, 1962), p. 46.

11. D. W. Waters, *The Art of Navigation in England in Elizabethan and Early Stuart Times* (New Haven, 1958), p. 82.

12. *Ibid.*, p. 146.

13. K. N. Chaudhuri, *The English East India Company* (London, 1965), pp. 23–28.

14. Abdul Amin, *British Interests in the Persian Gulf, 1747–1778* (unpublished dissertation, University of Maryland, 1962), pp. 7–8.

15. Percival Griffiths, *The British Impact in India* (London, 1952), p. 51.

16. *Ibid.*, p. 56.

17. *Ibid.*, p. 56.

18. *Ibid.*, p. 58.

19. Thomas Babington Macaulay, *Critical and Historical Essays* (London: Everyman Library, 1907), I, 487–88.

20. J. W. Fortescue, *A History of the British Army* (London, 1935), II, 597.

21. Lewis Mumford, *Technics and Civilization* (New York, 1934), p. 88.

22. *The Times* (London), July 16, 1857, p. 9 (Despatch from Punjab, May 28, 1857).

23. David Thompson, "The United Kingdom and its World-Wide Interests," *The New Cambridge Modern History*, X (London, 1960), 349.

24. David S. Landes, "Technological Change and Development in Western Europe, 1750–1914," *The Cambridge Economic History of Europe*, VI, Part I (Cambridge, 1965), 353.

25. *Principal Speeches and Addresses of H. R. H. The Prince Consort* (London, 1862), pp. 110–12, quoted in J. F. C. Harrison, ed., *Society and Politics in England, 1780–1960* (New York, 1965), p. 211.

26. J. H. Newman, *Parochial and Lay Sermons*, 8, No. 11, 159, quoted in Walter E. Houghton, *The Victorian Frame of Mind* (New Haven, 1957), p. 183.

27. Thomas Babington Macaulay, in Hugh Trevor-Roper, ed., *Critical and Historical Essays* (New York, 1965), p. 168.

28. *The Complete Writings of Ralph Waldo Emerson* (New York, 1929), Vol. I, 428.

29. *Ibid.*, p. 447.

30. *Ibid.*, p. 427.

31. Arthur Arberry, *Asiatic Jones: The Life and Influence of Sir William Jones* (London, 1964), p. 34.

32. Quoted in Kenneth Stunkel, *Indian Ideas and Western Thought During the Romantic Age* (Unpublished dissertation, University of Maryland, 1966), p. 87.

33. Klaus E. Knorr, *British Colonial Theories, 1570–1850* (Toronto, 1944), p. 380.

34. Richard Faber, *The Vision and the Need* (London, 1966), p. 39.

35. Thomas Carlyle, *Chartism*, quoted in Faber, *op. cit.*, p. 63.

36. J. A. Froude, *The English in the West Indies* (London, 1888), p 182, quoted in Faber, *op. cit.*, p. 62.

37. Michael Edwardes, *High Noon of Empire* (London, 1965), p. 15.

38. C. H. Philips, "James Mill, Mountstuart Elphinstone and the History of India," in C. H. Philips, ed., *Historians of India, Pakistan and Ceylon* (London, 1961), p. 221.

39. *The Spectator*, Jan. 11, 1868, quoted in C. A. Bodelson, *Studies in Mid-Victorian Imperialism* (Copenhagen, 1924), p. 127 footnote.

40. R. K. Das Gupta, "Macaulay's Writings on India," in Philips, ed., *op. cit.*, p. 236.

41. George Bennett, ed., *Concept of Empire* (London, 1953), p. 70.

42. *Ibid.*, p. 356.

Chapter 2

1. Arthur Berriedale Keith, *The Sovereignty of the British Dominions* (London, 1929), p. 277.
2. Barrington Moore, Jr., *Social Origins of Dictatorship and Democracy* (Boston, 1966), p. 35.
3. Helen Taft Manning, *The British Empire After the American Revolution* (New Haven, 1933), p. 72.
4. Gerald M. Craig, ed., *Lord Durham's Report* (Carleton Library ed., Toronto, 1963), p. 144.
5. Percival Spear, *A History of India,* Vol. II (Baltimore, 1965), 155.
6. Donald G. Creighton, "The Victorians and the Empire," in R. L. Schuyler and H. Ausubel, *The Making of English History* (New York, 1952), p. 555.
7. John Gallagher and Ronald Robinson, "The Imperialism of Free Trade," *Economic History Review,* 2nd ser., VI (August, 1953), 1–15.
8. Lord Palmerston, Minute, "Protection of Trade," April 22, 1860, F/02/34, in C. W. Newbury, *British Policy towards West Africa, 1786–1874* (Oxford, 1965), p. 120.
9. Donald Southgate, *The Most English Prime Minister* (New York, 1966), p. 144.
10. Herman Ausubel, *John Bright, Victorian Reformer* (New York, 1966), p. 42.
11. Adam Smith, *The Wealth of Nations* (Modern Library ed. New York, 1937), p. 431.
12. *Ibid.,* p. 573.
13. *Ibid.,* p. 581.
14. Donald Winch, *Classical Political Economy and Colonies* (Cambridge, Mass., 1965), pp. 46–47.
15. Earl Grey, *The Colonial Policy of Lord John Russell's Administration* (London, 1853), pp. 10–11, as quoted in C. A. Bodelsen, *Studies in Mid-Victorian Imperialism* (Copenhagen, 1924), p. 35.
16. *Ibid.*
17. *Ibid.,* p. 45.
18. J. H. Rose, A. P. Newton, E. A. Benians, eds., *The Cambridge History of the British Empire,* II (Cambridge, 1940), viii.
19. Creighton, *op. cit.,* p. 558.
20. John Strachey, *The End of Empire* (New York, 1960), p. 98.
21. Charles Dilke, *Greater Britain,* Vol. II (London, 1868), 151.

Chapter 3

1. Robert L. Schuyler, *Parliament and the British Empire* (New York, 1929), p. 220. The authority quoted was Sir Charles Lucas, a high-ranking Colonial Office civil servant.
2. Great Britain, *Statutes at Large,* XXXII/4, 18 George III, C. 12.
3. Sir Charles Wood to Sir Charles Trevelyan, Aug. 17, 1864. India Office Library, Eur. Mss. F. 78, India Office Letter Bk. #18.
4. B. J. Dalton, "Governor Browne and the Service Chiefs," *The Australian Journal of Politics and History,* Vol. XIII, No. 2 (August 1967), 232.
5. Paul Knaplund, *James Stephen and the British Colonial System, 1813–1847,* (Madison, Wisconsin, 1953), p. 278.

6. Sir Anton Bertram, *The Colonial Service* (Cambridge, 1930), pp. 68–69.

7. William R. Roff, *The Origins of Malay Nationalism* (New Haven, 1967), p. 11.

8. H. E. Egerton, ed., *Selected Speeches of Sir William Molesworth* (London, 1903), p. 247.

9. Brian Bond, ed., *Victorian Military Campaigns* (New York, 1967), p. 12.

10. *Ibid.*, p. 28.

11. Christopher Lloyd, *The Nation and the Navy* (London, 1954), p. 237.

Chapter 4

1. B. R. Mitchell and Phyllis Deane, *Abstract of British Historical Statistics* (Cambridge, 1962), p. 6.

2. J. D. B. Miller, *Britain and the Old Dominions* (Baltimore, 1966), pp. 15–16.

3. Brinley Thomas, *Migration and Economic Growth* (Cambridge, 1954), p. 57.

4. David S. Landes, "Technological Change and Development in Western Europe, 1750–1914," *The Cambridge Economic History of Europe*, Vol. VI, The Industrial Revolutions and After: Incomes, Population and Technological Change (I) (Cambridge, 1965), p. 353.

5. Maurice Collis, *Foreign Mud: The Opium Imbroglio in Canton in the 1830's and the Anglo-Chinese War that Followed* (New York, 1947), p. 80.

6. Arthur Birnie, *An Economic History of the British Isles* (London, 1935, University Paperbacks ed. 1961), p. 268.

7. Leland H. Jenks, *The Migration of British Capital to 1875* (New York, 1938), p. 36.

8. *Ibid.*, p. 95.

9. William Ashworth, *A Short History of the International Economy, 1850–1950* (London, 1952), p. 70.

10. J. A. Hobson, *Imperialism* (London, 1905), p. 48.

11. *Ibid.*, p. 49.

12. R. Robinson, J. Gallagher, and A. Denny, *Africa and the Victorians* (London, 1961), p. 472.

13. William Roger Louis, "Great Britain and the African Peace Settlement of 1919," *American Historical Review*, Vol. LXXI, No. 3 (April, 1966), p. 892.

14. Adam Smith, *op. cit.*, pp. 531–32.

15. S. Radhakrishnan, *Eastern Religions and Western Thought* (London, 1939), p. 257.

16. Morris D. Morris, "Towards a Reinterpretation of Nineteenth Century Indian Economic History," *Journal of Economic History*, Vol. XXIII, No. 4 (December, 1963), p. 611.

17. Sir Charles Trevelyan to Sir Charles Wood, March 4, 1863. India Office Library, Eur. Mss. F. 78/59/5–6.

18. D. C. M. Platt, *Finance, Trade, and Politics in British Foreign Policy 1815–1914* (Oxford, 1968), p. 88.

19. Mohandas K. Gandhi, *Hind Swaraj* (Ahmedabad, 1946), p. 73, quoted in Mary Matossian, "Ideologies of Delayed Industrialization: Some Tensions and Ambiguities," in Jason L. Finkle and Richard W. Gable, eds., *Political Development and Social Change* (New York, 1966), p. 178.

20. C. H. Allen, "The Industrialization of the Far East," H. J. Habakkuk and M. Postan, eds., *The Cambridge Economic History of Europe*, Vol. VI, Part II, 915.

21. Gunnar Myrdal, *Asian Drama: An Inquiry into the Poverty of Nations* (New York, 1968, Pantheon Book ed.), Vol. I, 581–82.

Chapter 5

1. Percival Spear, *The Nabobs* (London, 1963), p. 137.
2. *Ibid.*, p. 139.
3. *Edinburgh Review* (American ed.), Vol. 99 (July, 1853), p. 24.
4. Quoted in R. C. Majumbar, "Nationalist Historians," in C. H. Philips, ed., *Historians of India, Pakistan and Ceylon* (London, 1963), p. 417.
5. *Ibid.*, p. 418.
6. *Ibid.*
7. R. C. Majumdar, ed., *The History and Culture of the Indian People* (Bombay, 1965), Vol. 10, Part II, 466.
8. E. Daniel Potts, *British Baptist Missionaries in India, 1795–1837* (Cambridge, 1967), p. 210.
9. *Ibid.*, p. 212.
10. William Stanton, *The Leopard's Spots: Scientific Attitudes towards Race in America, 1815–59* (Pheonix ed., Chicago, 1966), p. 2.
11. David Brion Davis, *The Problem of Slavery in Western Culture* (Ithaca, 1966), p. 457.
12. *Ibid.*, p. 480. For the opinions of Captain James Cook and Joseph Banks, see J. C. Baaglehole, *The Endeavour Journal of Sir Joseph Banks*, Vol. I, parts II & III (Sydney, 1962), and James Cook, *A Journal of a Voyage Round the World in HMS Endeavour* (London 1771, facsimile ed. Amsterdam, 1967).
13. Stephen Neill, *Colonialism and Christian Missions* (New York, 1966), pp. 88–91.
14. James Morris, *Pax Britannica: Climax of an Empire* (London, 1968), p. 140.
15. Thomas R. Metcalfe, *The Aftermath of Revolt: India 1857–70* (Princeton, 1964), pp. 304–5.
16. Richard Faber, *The Vision and the Need* (London, 1966), p. 64.
17. W. David McIntyre, *The Imperial Frontier in the Tropics* (London, 1967), pp. 71–72.
18. George Bennett, ed., *Concept of Empire* (London, 1953), pp. 74–75.
19. The quotation is from Mr. Woodruffs' *Men Who Ruled India: The Guardians* (see Suggested Readings). But instances of brutality by British soldiers towards Indians were more frequent than Mr. Woodruff indicates. See Frank Richards' *Old-Soldier Sahib*, one of the few accounts of service in India written by a private soldier.
20. India Office Library, India Council Minutes, Vol. II, Frere minute, Feb. 18, 1868, pp. 430–36.
21. Sir John Kaye, *History of the Indian Mutiny* (new ed., London, 1897), Vol. I, 153–54.
22. W. K. Hancock, *Survey of British Commonwealth Affairs* (Oxford, 1937), Vol. I, p. 169.
23. Roland Oliver and J. D. Fage, *A Short History of Africa* (Baltimore, 1962), p. 98.
24. Report of the Committee on Aborigines, Great Britain, *Parliamentary Papers,* 1837, vii (425), quoted in Philip Curtin, *The Image of Africa* (Madison, Wisc. 1964), p. 458.
25. Robert I. Rotberg, *A Political History of Tropical Africa* (New York, 1965), p. 203.
26. D. H. Jones, book review in *Journal of African History*, Vol. 8, no. 1, 1967, 177.
27. Lugard had been born in India and had tried, but failed, to enter the Indian Civil Service.
28. Jomo Kenyatta, *Facing Mount Kenya* (New York, 1955), p. 305.

Chapter 6

1. W. B. Yeats, *Selected Poetry*, E. Norman Jeffares, ed. (London, 1962), p. 95.
2. Charles Dilke, *Greater Britain*, Vol. II (London, 1868), 151.
3. Quoted in Max Warren, *The Missionary Movement from Britain in Modern History* (London, 1965), pp. 75–76.

Suggested Readings

The books on this list have been chosen on the basis of their pertinence to the topics discussed in each of the chapters. Additional titles are provided in the *General and Bibliographical* section.

General and Bibliographical

Benians, E. A., Butler, Sir James, and Carrington, C. E. (eds.) *The Cambridge History of the British Empire* (8 vols.), Cambridge, 1929–63.

Carrington, C. E. *The British Overseas*, Cambridge, 1950.

Fieldhouse, D. K. *The Colonial Empires: A Comparative Study from the Eighteenth Century*, London, 1966.

Koebner, Richard *Empire*, London, 1961.

───── and Schmidt, H. D. *Imperialism, the Story and Significance of a Political Word*, London, 1964.

Robinson, R., Gallagher, J., and Denny, A. *Africa and the Victorians*, London, 1961.

Thornton, A. P. *Doctrines of Imperialism*, New York, 1965.

───── *The Imperial Idea and its Enemies*, London, 1959.

Winks, Robin W. (ed.) *The Historiography of the British Empire-Commonwealth*, Durham, N.C., 1966.

Chapter 1: The Roots of Power

Chauduri, K. N. *The English East India Company: the Study of an Early Joint Stock Company, 1600–1640*, London, 1965.

Cipolla, Carlo M. *Guns, Sails and Empires: Technological Innovation and the Early Phases of European Expansion, 1400–1700*, New York, 1965.

Davis, Ralph *The Rise of the English Shipping Industry in the Seventeenth and Eighteenth Centuries*, London, 1962.

Lach, Donald *Asia in the Making of Europe*, Chicago, 1965.

Landes, David S. "Technological Change and Development in Western Europe, 1750–1914." *The Cambridge Economic History of Europe*, VI, Pt. 1, Cambridge, 1965.

Panikkar, K. M. *Asia and Western Dominance*, London, 1953.

Waters, D. W. *The Art of Navigation in England in Elizabethan and Early Stuart Times*, New Haven, 1958.

White, Lynn *Medieval Technology and Social Change*, New York, 1962.

Chapter 2: The Limitations of Power

Bennett, George (ed.) *Concept of Empire*, London, 1953.

Bodelson, C. A. *Studies in Mid-Victorian Imperialism*, Copenhagen, 1924.

Dawson, R. M. *The Development of Dominion Status*, Toronto, 1937.

Knorr, Klaus *British Colonial Theories, 1570–1850*, London, 1944.

Porter, Bernard *Critics of Empire*, New York, 1968.

Schuyler, Robert L. *The Fall of the Old Colonial System*, New York, 1945.

Semmel, Bernard *Imperialism and Social Reform*, London, 1960.

Tyler, J. E. *The Struggle for Imperial Unity, 1868–1895*, London, 1938.

Winch, Donald *Classical Political Economy and Colonies*, Cambridge, Mass., 1965.

Chapter 3: The Apparatus of Power

Benians, E. A., Butler, Sir James, and Carrington, C. E. (eds.) *The Cambridge History of the British Empire*, Vol. III, Cambridge, 1959.

Bertram, A. *The Colonial Service*, Cambridge, 1930.

Bond, Brian *Victorian Military Campaigns*, New York, 1967.

Braibanti, Ralph (ed.) *Asian Bureaucratic Systems Emergent from the British Imperial Tradition*, Durham, N.C., 1966.

Frykenburg, Robert E. *Guntur District, 1788–1848*, Oxford, 1965.

Gordon, Donald C. *The Dominion Partnership in Imperial Defense, 1870–1914*, Baltimore, 1965.

Graham, G. S. *The Politics of Naval Supremacy*, Oxford, 1965.

———— *Great Britain in the Indian Ocean, 1810–1850*, Oxford, 1968.

Jeffries, Charles *The Colonial Office*, New York, 1956.

Knaplund, Paul *James Stephen and the British Colonial System*, Madison, Wisc., 1952.

Marder, Arthur J. *The Anatomy of British Sea Power, 1880–1905*, New York, 1940.

O'Malley, L. S. S. *The Indian Civil Service*, London, 1931.

Preston, Antony and Major, John *Send a Gunboat*, London, 1967.

Roth, William R. *The Origins of Malay Nationalism*, New Haven, 1967.

Schuyler, Robert L. *Parliament and the British Empire*, New York, 1920.

Woodruff, Philip *The Men Who Ruled India*, Vol. II, New York, 1954.

Chapter 4: The Economics of Power

Ashworth, William *A Short History of the International Economy*, London, 1952.

Cairncross, A. K. *Home and Foreign Investment, 1870–1913*, Cambridge, 1953.

Clark, G. Kitson *The Making of Victorian England*, London, 1963.

———— *An Expanding Society: Britain 1830–1900*, Cambridge, 1967.

Fieldhouse, D. K. " 'Imperialism'; An Historiographical Revision," *Economic History Review*, 2nd ser., XIV, 1961.

Gallagher, J. and Robinson, R. "The Imperialism of Free Trade," *Economic History Review*, 2nd ser., VI, No. 1, 1953.

Hobson, J. A. *Imperialism, a Study*, London, 1904.

Imlah, A. H. *Economic Elements in the Pax Britannica*, Cambridge, Mass., 1958.

Jenks, J. H. *The Migration of British Capital to 1875*, London, 1938.

Lenin, V. I. *Imperialism: The Highest Stage of Capitalism*, rev. trans. 2nd ed. New York, 1934.

Macdonagh, O. "The Anti-Imperialism of Free Trade," *Economic History Review*, 2nd ser., XIV, 1961.

Morris, Morris D. "Towards a Reinterpretation of Nineteenth Century Indian Economic History," *Journal of Economic History*, XXIII, No. 4, 1963.

Platt, D. C. M. *Finance, Trade and Politics: British Foreign Policy, 1815–1914*, Oxford, 1968.

Saul, S. B. *Studies in British Overseas Trade, 1870–1914*, Liverpool, 1960.

Winks, Robin W. *British Imperialism: Gold, God, Glory*, New York, 1963.

Chapter 5. The Arrogance of Power

Basham, A. L. *The Wonder that Was India*, London, 1954.

Curtin, Philip D. *The Image of Africa: British Ideas and Action, 1780–1850*, Madison, Wisc., 1965.

Davis, David Brion *The Problem of Slavery in Western Culture*, Ithaca, 1966.

Flint, John E. *Nigeria and Ghana*, Englewood Cliffs, N.J., 1966.

Griffith, Percival *The British Impact on India*, London, 1952.

Hutchins, Francis *The Illusion of Permanence: British Imperialism in India*, Princeton, 1967.

Ingham, Kenneth *Reformers in India, 1793–1833*, Cambridge, 1956.

Kenyatta, Jomo *Facing Mount Kenya*, New York, 1955.

McIntyre, W. David *The Imperial Frontier in the Tropics*, London, 1967.

Mehrotra, S. R. *India and the Commonwealth, 1885–1929*, London, 1965.

Metcalf, Thomas R. *The Aftermath of Revolt: India 1857–1870*, Princeton, 1964.

Neill, Stephen *Colonialism and Christian Missions*, New York, 1966.

Oliver, Roland *The Missionary Factor in East Africa*, London, 1952.

——— and Atmore, A. *Africa since 1800*, Cambridge, 1967.

Potts, E. Daniel *British Baptist Missionaries in India, 1795–1837*, Cambridge, 1967.

Rotberg, Robert I. *A Political History of Tropical Africa*, New York, 1965.

Spear, Percival *The Nabobs*, London, 1931.

Stokes, Eric *The English Utilitarians and India*, Oxford, 1959.

Chapter 6: The Decline of Power

Cross, Colin *The Fall of the British Empire*, London, 1968.
Menon, V. P. *The Transfer of Power in India*, London, 1957.
Perham, Margery *The Colonial Reckoning*, London, 1961.
Strachey, John *The End of Empire*, New York, 1959.
Tinker, Hugh *Experiment in Freedom: India and Pakistan, 1947*, London, 1967.

Index

Date Due